Other Titles of Interest

An introduction
to the World Wide Web
for PC and Mac users

by

**Daniel, Christine
and
Owen Bishop**

**BERNARD BABANI (publishing) LTD
THE GRAMPIANS
SHEPHERDS BUSH ROAD
LONDON W6 7N
ENGLAND**

Please Note

Although every care has been taken with the production of this book to ensure that any projects, designs, modifications and/or programs, etc., contained herewith, operate in a correct and safe manner and also that any components specified are normally available in Great Britain, the Publishers and Author(s) do not accept responsibility in any way for the failure (including fault in design) of any projects, design, modification or program to work correctly or to cause damage to any equipment that it may be connected to or used in conjunction with, or in respect of any other damage or injury that may be so caused, nor do the Publishers accept responsibility in any way for the failure to obtain specified components.

Notice is also given that if equipment that is still under warranty is modified in any way or used or connected with home-built equipment then that warranty may be void.

© 1996 BERNARD BABANI (publishing) LTD

First Published – December 1996

British Library Cataloguing in Publication Data
A catalogue record for this book is available from the British Library

ISBN 0 85934 390 1

Cover Designed by Gregor Arthur
Cover Illustration by Adam Willis
Printed and Bound in Great Britain by Cox & Wyman Ltd, Reading

Preface

The Internet is a network of computers, which was founded in the USA in the 1970's, but has since grown to encompass over 30 million users in more than 80 countries worldwide. It now comprises a large number of commercial and non-commercial networks, and individual computers, which communicate using a set of standard computer languages. Since its inception, the Internet has been a valuable means of communication and a growing repository of information. The main drawback was that it was not very easy to use and access. Most users were scientists in government institutions, universities and the military. This has all changed with the advent of the World Wide Web, a system that provides easy access to the Internet for all, whether you are a university academic, a businessperson or are simply using a computer at home for a hobby. The World Wide Web is a multimedia tool, providing information in an attractive manner, page by page, in full colour, with pictures, sound and video clips, and is easily controlled, simply by using a computer mouse. There are now more than 70,000 computers worldwide dispensing information via the World Wide Web.

This book describes the World Wide Web revolution, and shows you how to join in, for the minimum cost and effort. In Chapter 1 we describe the origins of the World Wide Web, its relationship to the Internet, and the principles of its operation. We show you how you can connect to the World Wide Web, and discuss its potential to become the dominant force in the evolving Information Superhighway. In Chapter 2, we go on to describe the main features and capabilities of 'browser' programs, which are the programs we use to explore the World Wide Web. Other aspects of the Internet that you will encounter when using the World Wide Web are discussed in Chapter 3, such as electronic mail and Network News. Chapter 4 provides key starting points for your exploration of the World Wide Web, and lists some of the best software archives available on the Internet. Chapters 5, 6 and 7 describe links to some of the best commercial sites, sources of information and entertainment on the Web. We provide a summary of currently available World Wide Web 'browser' programs in Chapter 8, including the powerful *Netscape Navigator*, recently estimated to be used by

70% of those surfing the Web. Throughout this book we provide hints and tips for users of this program, which is the most popular browser currently available. In Chapter 9 there is also a short introduction to creating your own Web pages, including a guide to some of the software available to help you. At the end of the book there is a comprehensive glossary which explains in plain English the ever-increasing number of buzzwords and jargon. There is also a comprehensive list of Internet software suppliers and UK Internet vendors. A complete index of all the topics discussed in the book means you can quickly look things up.

The World Wide Web is also commonly known as 'WWW', 'W3' or simply as the 'Web'. In this book, for the sake of brevity, we will usually refer to the World Wide Web as the 'Web', but look out for the other abbreviations, which you will come across often in books, magazines and the Web itself.

D., C. & O. Bishop

About the Authors

Daniel, Christine and Owen were co-authors of the recently published book "An Introduction to Networks for PC and Mac Users" (BP373). In addition, Daniel Bishop has written over 30 articles for computer magazines. Owen Bishop is well known as a contributor to popular computing and electronics magazines and is author of over 60 books, mostly in computing and electronics.

Acknowledgements

Victoria University of Wellington are thanked for providing computing facilities during the writing of this book.

Trademarks

Microsoft, MS-DOS, Microsoft Word, Microsoft Word for Windows, Microsoft Excel, Microsoft Windows, Windows NT and *Windows 95* are registered trademarks of Microsoft Corporation. The term Windows, as used in this book, refers to Microsoft Windows.

IBM ,OS/2, OS/2 Warp and *WebExplorer* are registered trademarks of International Business Machines Corporation.

Apple, Macintosh, HyperCard, LocalTalk, and *Apple Remote Access* are registered trademarks of Apple Computer Incorporated.

Ethernet is a registered trademark of Digital Equipment Corporation, Intel and Xerox Corporation.

Unix is a registered trademark of AT&T.

Netscape, Netscape Navigator, and *Secure Courier* are registered trademarks of Netscape Communications Corporation.

WordPerfect and *NetWare* are registered trademarks of Novell Incorporated.

All other trademarks are the registered and legally protected trademarks of the companies who make the products. There is no intent to use the trademarks generically and readers should investigate ownership of a trademark before using it for any purpose.

Contents

Chapter 1

WHAT IS THE WORLD WIDE WEB?

The Web
The World Wide Web is a relatively new phenomenon for many people, even for the growing number who have already heard about or use the better-known Internet. For many, there is still confusion about what it is. The World Wide Web is not synonymous with the Internet, but rather is a new feature of the Internet. Neither is it a Bulletin Board System, although it offers some similar services. Nor is it a type of Local Area Network (LAN) or a Wide Area Network (WAN). It is in fact a communication protocol, or simple computer language, meant for creating, storing and retrieving information over a large network of computers such as the Internet. However, a Web user does not even need to know this much. The Web has been designed to be extremely easy to use – much easier than using a video machine, for example! Once you have started the Web program on your computer, all you need to do is to select what you want by moving the pointer across the screen with your mouse, and press the mouse button. Many happy hours can be spent by simply moving your mouse and 'clicking' the mouse button, to grab pages of information. However, to really get the most from the Web, it helps to have an understanding of what it is and how it works. As you will discover, there is already almost 'too much' information available via the Web, and one of the most important skills to learn is how to find what you really want, as quickly as possible, and by-pass all the rest.

In this chapter we introduce you to the fundamental concepts of the Web, and describe exactly what we mean by this term. We also look at what you need to access the Web on your computer, and what costs may be involved.

The Internet
Before we can discuss the Web itself, we must firstly understand what has made the development of the Web possible. The Web depends on the existence of large computer networks, and in particular, the best-known worldwide network, which is called the

Internet. The basic concepts of computer networks and the Internet are discussed in this section.

Computers which are linked together by cables or other means, and which can communicate with each other, form what are called networks. Computer networks were first constructed in the very early days of computer development in the 1950's and 60's, usually to connect two or more large computers and their terminals, i.e. keyboards and monitors which could be used to enter and display data. Since then, a huge number of networks of different types and sizes have been created. Computer networks which occupy an office or a building are often called a Local Area Network or LAN for short. Larger networks which are almost entirely commercial, and which cover a larger geographical area, are called Wide Area Networks (WANs). Networks may be linked by dedicated and specialised electrical cables, such as the well-known *Ethernet* cable, extensively used for linking LANs. Alternatively the computers may be linked via standard telephone lines, or dedicated long-distance electrical or optical cables. It is becoming more and more common not to use physical connections, particularly for large networks, but to use radio, microwave and satellite links instead. Not only can networks be differentiated by how they are constructed, but also by how they are financed and who the main users are. Many networks are entirely private and commercial, such as those operated by large banks, news organisations, and airlines. Many offer access to members of the public and other organisations on the basis that they pay the specified charges for the use of the network. These are commonly known as Bulletin Board Systems (BBSs). Popular BBSs include CompuServe, eWorld, IBM Global Network, and The Microsoft Network. There are also non-profit, non-commercial networks, mainly designed to help academics to communicate and exchange information, such as the National Science Foundation Network (NSFNET) in the USA.

The Internet is also a computer network, but is quite different from all those mentioned above, because it comprises a large number of mostly non-commercial networks which have been joined together, thus it actually includes such networks as NSFNET in the USA, and many similar networks in other countries, such as the Joint Academic Network (JANET) in the UK. Networks such as NSFNET and JANET are integral to the structure of the Internet, and networks of this kind are often

2

referred to as 'backbone' networks. They provide essential support to the Internet, in the same way that the backbone does in a human body.

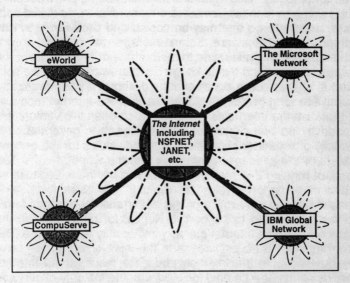

The Internet and its relationship to some other major networks

The history of the Internet can be traced back to the establishment of the Advanced Research Projects Agency Network (ARPANET) by the US Department of Defense in 1969. This network later became divided into the ARPANET and the Milnet, and it also spawned many other similar networks. These networks were connected to the ARPANET by a technology known as DARPA (Defense-ARPA). The ARPANET and connected networks became known collectively as the DARPA Internet, and eventually became known more simply as the 'Internet'. Since the 1970's the Internet has grown many fold, and now includes a large number of major networks around the world.

For many years the Internet has been used for communication between its users, who until recently have mainly consisted of university academics, government and military scientists. The most common form of communication is called electronic mail, or

'e-mail' for short, whereby messages are typed in by one user, relayed to another user who has a specific Internet address, and displayed on their screen for them to read. Another major use of the Internet has been the transfer of computer files, including data and program files, from one user to another, and from computer archives to individual users. Programs are also called software, and software that may be copied and used freely by any person is called 'freeware'. Some programs may be used provided a small donation is made to the authors or to a charity of the authors' choice, and this is known as shareware, since the software is 'shared'. Both e-mail and the distribution of freeware and shareware form two of the biggest uses of the Internet today.

Because the Internet is essentially a co-operative venture it is owned by no one person or organisation. It is governed by a number of volunteer committees and individuals for the general benefit of the academic community and the world at large. The costs of running the Internet are kept to a minimum because so much of the effort involved in running it is given freely, and because of the generosity of the governmental and academic bodies which help to support it. Hence, for many people, the costs of using the Internet are very low or may even be free. The 90's has seen a huge increase in the involvement of the commercial sector in the Internet, and as a result, some Internet services must now be paid for. However, the majority of services are still very low cost or free to many users.

Internet computers communicate and exchange data using a special computer communication language, or protocol, known as TCP/IP (Transmission Control Protocol / Internet Protocol). This is a very fundamental system, used also by many LANs and WANs. The Web also depends on TCP/IP. All software that uses the Internet or the Web must be able to use TCP/IP.

The advent of the Web has been a major leap forward for the Internet. It has made interacting with the Internet easy and enjoyable, particularly for Macintosh and PC users. Use of the Internet is no longer restricted to computer boffins. The Web has opened-up the Internet to a much wider audience than before, and promises to grow rapidly over the next few years.

The Evolution of the Web
The origins of the Web can be traced back to March 1989, when Tim Berners-Lee and Robert Cailliau at CERN (the European

Centre for Particle Physics) proposed a new networked database system designed to provide an easy way for users of a computer network to access the data and information distributed across the network. Systems for accessing networked data-bases had already been available for some time, but were relatively inflexible, clumsy to use, and unattractive in appearance, in comparison to the Web. The Web was originally meant only for use by researchers on high-energy physics collaborations, but this did not last long. In 1990 the name 'World Wide Web' was decided, and the first working system was developed on a computer system called NeXT. In 1991 the system was publicly demonstrated at the San Antonio Hypertext Conference in the USA. Work also began in 1991 on a Macintosh program for exploring the Web and viewing Web pages, called a 'browser', which was eventually released in January 1993. It was known originally as *MacWWW* and later as *Samba*. This program had very limited facilities and is now rarely used.

In 1991, Marc Andreessen and colleagues at the NCSA (National Center for Supercomputing Applications) in the USA, began work on another browser, known as *Mosaic*. A version for Unix computers was released in February 1993, and later that year, versions for both PCs and Macintoshes were released, which were free for anyone to use. As a result *Mosaic* became the most popular Web browser for PC and Macintosh users for the following two years. Also in 1993 the ability to send colour images via the Web was developed. The first commercial network to use the Web was CommerceNet, started in 1994. In March 1994, Marc Andreessen and several colleagues left NCSA to found a new company, Netscape Communications Corporation, with the aim of developing their own superior version of *Mosaic*. Usage of the Web increased dramatically in 1994, and for the first time the amount of traffic on the Internet due to the Web first exceeded that due to Gopher (see Chapter 3), which had until that time been the chief competitor to the Web. The First International WWW Conference took place in Geneva, Switzerland, in May 1994.

In late 1994 the *Netscape Navigator* program from Netscape Communications Corporation was released, and by early 1995 became the most popular and widely used program for interacting with the Web, overtaking its predecessor *Mosaic* and other Web programs which had appeared during 1994. The Second

International WWW Conference took place in Chicago, USA, in October 1994, and the third took place in Darmstadt, Germany, in April 1995. The fourth was held in Boston in December 1995.

Who runs it all?

The Web depends on the Internet for its existence, so we must firstly look at how the Internet is administered, before we go on to discuss the how the Web is run. The Internet is a co-operative venture between a vast number of mainly government and academic organisations around the world, who each run their own networks and their portions of the Internet. Its structure is complex and verging on the chaotic, since it has grown on an *ad hoc* basis over the years, without a great deal of advance planning. What this means, though, is that it is not too dependent on any one part of its structure, and cannot easily be controlled or dominated by any organisation, not that users of the Internet would allow it anyway! The Internet community are almost uniformly against any moves by external organisations to place controls or restrictions on the Internet.

Despite this, there is a need for the development of the Internet to be overseen, or 'steered'. If this were not done, then the system would eventually sink into irretrievable chaos, owing to non-standardisation and lack of co-operation. Developments in the Internet are usually brought about by volunteer committees and work groups, and decisions taken at international Internet conferences. One of the most important organisations is the Internet Society (ISOC), which was founded in 1992 in the USA, but is now a global organisation. Its objectives are standardisation of the Internet, promoting the use of the Internet, and the development of new Internet technology and software. The ISOC oversees several work groups, the best known of which is the IAB (Internet Activities Board), which in turn oversees the IETF (Internet Engineering Task Force) and the IRTF (Internet Research Task Force). The IAB's main role is in the definition of Internet standards, for both hardware and software. The IEFT spends much of its time looking at current problems and shortcomings of the Internet, and tries to solve them. The IRTF concentrates on the long-term and future development of the Internet. The task of assigning Internet code numbers is delegated by the IAB to the IANA (Internet Assigned Numbers Authority). Internet addresses are assigned and distributed by

the NIC (Network Information Center). NIC is now administered by SRI International, a Californian contract research firm, originally founded in 1946 in conjunction with Stanford University as the Stanford Research Institute.

The most important mechanism for Internet management is the RFC (Request For Comment) system. RFCs are written by those who wish to make changes to the Internet, or to clarify certain aspects, and these may or may not be accepted by the IAB. Once accepted, RFCs get a catalogue number, and may be retrieved via the Internet by anyone who is interested, from a number of different computer archives. RFCs are guidelines only, and not mandatory, but if the Internet is to function smoothly, it is best that the RFCs are adhered to.

Governments can also exert influence on the Internet by virtue of the fact that many of the key parts of the Internet depend on national government funded bodies, such as universities and other research institutions. By controlling funding, governments can substantially affect the Internet. For example, until recently, the NSFNET (National Science Foundation Network) was the official main backbone network of the Internet in the USA. The NSF (National Science Foundation) was in a position of power over the Internet, particularly during the early development of the Internet, when Internet usage was predominantly confined to the USA. However, the US government has recently withdrawn much of the funding for support of the Internet by the NSF. As a result, a miscellany of other organisations are starting to manage the Internet in the USA, in place of the NSF, such as IDT (International Discount Telecommunications).

Some governments have tried to regulate the Internet directly, although their efforts are commonly misguided and attract condemnation from the Internet community. For example, at the time of writing, the New Zealand government had put forward proposals which would make it illegal for any Internet carrier or relay agency to carry 'objectionable' material, such as pornography. Such laws are not easily workable, since it is impractical for an Internet carrier to monitor or censor the huge amount of information that it handles. Trying to censor what is carried by the Internet would be rather like trying to censor what is sent through the ordinary post, which would involve opening and checking every envelope and parcel. Not only would it be highly impractical, it would also be a major infringement of personal

privacy. Instead, it would be more practical for the law to target the producers and receivers of objectionable material on the Internet.

The structure of the Internet, and particularly its international links, may also be affected by decisions of the world's large telecommunication companies. Much of the Internet traffic is carried by them, and hence the routes they use and the tariffs they charge affect the Internet.

As mentioned earlier, the original development of the Web was controlled by CERN. However, in 1995 the development of the Web was transferred from CERN to a new organisation known as the International World Wide Web Consortium (W3C), run by the Laboratory for Computer Science at MIT (Massachusetts Institute of Technology) in the USA, CERN and INRIA (Institut National de Recherche en Informatique et en Automatique) in Europe. As well as steering the development of the Web by carrying out its own research and creating standards, the consortium also organises international conferences at least once every year, for discussion of issues affecting the Web. The last one was held in Boston in December 1995.

The Web is also strongly influenced by Web users and what they make available, and the developers of Web software. For example, owing to the popularity of the *Netscape Navigator* Web program from Netscape Communications, many Web pages are now designed to be specifically compatible with the *Netscape Navigator* program.

Thus the development of both the Internet and the Web is partly a result of steering by voluntary groups, and partly a result of the influence of Internet users and other individuals, governments and large corporations. What is important to realise is that no one person or organisation has overall control or monopoly on either the Internet or the Web, meaning that the costs are kept to a minimum and the medium is relatively unregulated and free to develop. This basic principle is probably well worth protecting. Dominance by any one organisation, government or company could easily lead to a more restricted and expensive Internet, and make using the Web much less appealing.

8

Hypertext

Hypertext is a method of storing information on a computer as a collection of text documents, which are linked to one another by keywords embedded in the body of the text, known as 'links', or sometimes as 'anchors'. These links are highlighted in every hypertext document. Web programs typically show these links by using a different colour from the rest of the text, by underlining them, or they may have a number beside them. A link may be selected by pointing a mouse and clicking the mouse button, or by entering the number of the link.

For example, a typical hypertext sentence may look something like this:

"In this issue of our Web magazine, we discuss <u>modems</u>, and list the latest <u>hot Web sites</u>."

We have two links to choose from. By selecting the link word '*modems*' we might receive a new unit of hypertext:

"There are several new modems on the market, which we compare on the basis of <u>price</u>, <u>performance</u>, and <u>ease of use</u>."

Again, we can select any one of the links to get more information. Essentially, hypertext is text which contains links to other texts. Some links can lead back to previous texts, providing a way for the user to back-track. Such links are called 'back-links'.

Hypertext documents are sometimes called 'nodes'. The nodes and their links are collectively called a 'web', hence explaining how the World Wide Web got its name.

In theory, a hypertext document may have any length, from just a few words to hundreds of pages, although they are typically about one page long, or one computer screenful of information. This amount of hypertext is called a 'hypertext page'.

The hypertext concept is actually much older than the Web. The term was coined around 1965 by Ted Nelson in California, to describe what he called "non-sequential writing". The first major application of hypertext to personal computing was Apple Computers' *Hypercard* program, released for Macintoshes in 1987. Hypercard is a personal computer database, which uses

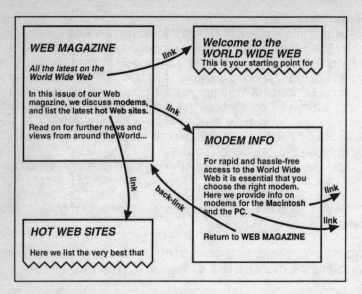

Typical hypertext documents, links to other documents, and back-links

the hypertext concept to store and retrieve information. Text and graphics are stored on so-called 'cards' which may be displayed by the computer. Cards are another example of a type of hypertext node. Other media may be accessed through special extensions to *Hypercard*. The user can then move from one card to another by selecting the highlighted links. Although some purists claimed that this was not a proper hypertext system, this product greatly increased the popularity of hypertext, prior to its adoption by CERN in 1989 for the Web.

The hypertext method is also used in the Microsoft *Windows* help system, which will be familiar to many readers. Users can move from topic to topic by selecting highlighted words or phrases, which act to link the many help pages together.

Since the hypertext method was conceived, it has been expanded to include images, video and sound, as well as just text. This is then called hypermedia, which can be compared with the term multimedia (see below). It has become quite common use the term hypertext to mean hypermedia, although strictly this is not correct. In hypermedia, links may not just consist of

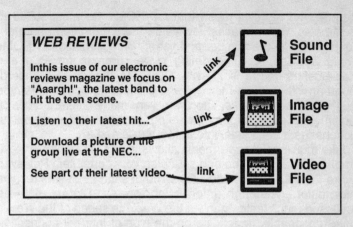

A hypertext document and links to hypermedia resources

words, but may be graphical symbols, such as buttons or icons, or even pictures.

Hypermedia and Multimedia
Hypermedia, although developed from the concept of hypertext, as described above, also bears comparison with another phenomenon of the '90s, which is multimedia. Hypermedia and multimedia both involve presentation of text, graphics, pictures, video and sound on personal computers. Whilst hypermedia is available through the Web, multimedia is made available using compact data storage devices, particularly CD-ROMs.

Multimedia has only become possible because of the rapid advances in computer hardware technology and the development of CD-ROMs over the last 5–10 years, which means that personal computers can store very large amounts of data, and retrieve it very quickly when required. These factors are very important for multimedia to be viable. Text and other media can be coded for use on a computer system, but only text can be coded in a really compact manner. Code for graphics, pictures, video and sound is always much greater in size than for text. Older PCs, such as 286 and even some 386 machines are not really suitable for multimedia, nor are old Macintoshes, such as Classics. They take too long to retrieve data, and may not have sufficient space to store the data, either in memory or on hard disc. The requirements for high speed and high volume data

storage and retrieval mean that CD-ROMs are most suited to multimedia. Within the last few years there has been a tremendous growth in the number and variety of multimedia CD-ROMs available. Also, it is becoming more common for PCs and Macintoshes to be sold with CD-ROM drives as standard, together with enough memory and processing power to handle multimedia applications. There are very many different types of multimedia applications, including games, encyclopaedias, dictionaries, catalogues, interactive music and art.

Like multimedia, hypermedia allows you to view complex text, graphics, images, video and sound on your computer. However, unlike CD-ROMs, the Web allows you to send as well as receive information. Although information on CD-ROMs may be accessed much faster than via the Web, the speed of the Web is quite reasonable, depending on the type of Internet connection you are using. More importantly, the information on the Web is generally being updated all the time, unlike a CD-ROM. Also, at any one time the amount of information available on the Web is orders of magnitude greater than that available on any CD-ROM, and most of it is free too.

The hypertext and hypermedia pages which are to be found on the Web are created using a special language, called HTML (Hypertext Mark-up Language). This comprises a number of simple codes which define the appearance of Web pages, particularly the layout of text and graphics, titles, subheadings, bold and italic text. Perhaps most importantly, HTML also encodes the links to other Web pages and Internet resources.

Web pages and other kinds of data are transferred from one computer to another on the Internet using a special communications system, especially developed for the Web, called HTTP (Hypertext Transfer Protocol). However, HTTP cannot manage without TCP/IP, the fundamental communications language of the Internet, as well as most LANs and WANs.

Clients and Servers
In any computer network there will be exchange of information between the computers within that network. A computer that supplies information may be called a server, and a computer that receives that information may be called a client. Most computers can act either as a client or a server computer. However, in most networks, including most LANs, one or more computers are

specially set-up as servers, and as such, they serve all the other computers on the network, which are the clients. Servers provide access to information and resources, such as hardware devices like printers, hard discs, and scanners, and possibly links to other networks.

Servers and clients also exist in the context of the Internet. There are a large number of computers on the Internet which are set up to be servers, providing Internet users with access to the data and resources that are on the server computer. Access may be by a variety of methods, such as the Web. The computers which are used to access the server can be called clients, and the software used to do the job can be called client software, or a client program. The user can enter requests for information using the client software, which then passes on the request to the server via the Internet. Software on the server computer, called server software, recognises the request, finds the required information, and returns it via the Internet. The client software then recognises the incoming information, and displays it on the client computer's screen, or saves it onto a disc. Thus, client software provides a means for users of the Internet to interact with server computers on the Internet.

Recent estimates indicate that there are more than 70,000 computers connected to the Internet that provide Web pages. There are two main methods of accessing and reading these Web pages.

Firstly, there are a few specially set-up computers on the Internet that provide a Web access service, which allows you access to the remaining 70,000 plus Web servers. These Web access services are themselves accessed by using a very simple method of Internet connection known as Telnet. A Telnet connection will give you a text-only display, but nothing more. Most Web pages can be viewed and understood in text-only mode, but clearly you miss out on quite a lot, particularly the images, sound and video which are available, and really an integral part of the Web. More detail on connecting to the Web using the Telnet method is given in Chapter 3.

Most users of the Web do not use the Telnet method, since you lose almost all the special hypermedia features and interactive aspects of the Web. Instead, most Web users access the 70,000 plus Web servers more directly, by using a specially designed Web client program. There are currently a large

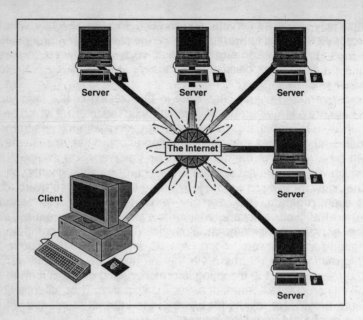

A client computer can link to many servers via the Internet

number widely available for both Macintoshes and PCs. Web client programs are also commonly called 'browsers', since they provide the user with the ability to browse through pages of information available on the Web. They are also sometimes called 'navigators' because they enable the user to find their way through the Web and explore the Internet. In this book we will refer to many types of browsers, and describe how they work.

Connection to the Internet

All the browsers mentioned in this book require that you have a Macintosh or PC which has direct access to the Internet. By direct access, we mean using a TCP/IP connection, either via a LAN that is connected to the Internet, or via a modem to an Internet host computer.

LANs usually connect to the Internet using dedicated high-speed lines which means that as a Web user you will get much faster access to Web pages and other Internet resources. Such lines may be special electrical or optical fibre cables, and are typ-

ically leased from telecommunications companies. They are very costly, although they can be quite economic if shared amongst many LAN users. In contrast, users of modems will find the Web much slower, being limited by the speed of their modem. Also, telephone cables are simply not capable of moving large amounts of data as fast as dedicated cables, but on the other hand, are a fraction of the cost.

If you use a LAN, the physical connection between your PC or Macintosh and the LAN will normally be via special network wiring, such as *Ethernet* or Apple *LocalTalk* cables. Computers on the network will typically communicate using TCP/IP. Commonly used TCP/IP programs include *MacTCP*, which is provided freely by Apple Computers for Macintoshes, and Trumpet *Winsock* for *Windows* users, a shareware program from Trumpet Software International.

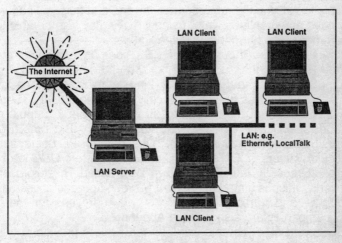

Connecting to the Internet via a LAN

Most individual users of the Web and the Internet use a modem connected to their PC or Macintosh. The modem can connect your computer to an Internet host computer that also has a modem, and has been set up to provide Internet access. Such Internet host computers with dial-in access are often provided for use by staff and students at educational institutions,

and in some countries by local government bodies for use by the general public. For example, free dial-in Internet access is provided by some local city councils in New Zealand.

There are also many commercial Internet providers to choose from (also called Internet vendors). Many users of the Web gain access by using the services of a commercial Internet vendor. Popular Internet vendors in the UK include Demon Internet, Hiway, and Unipalm-PIPEX, but there are many others, some of which are listed in Appendix 3.

BBSs provide a variety of services, which will commonly include limited access to the Internet. Owing to the rising popularity of the Web, many BBS companies now provide their customers with access to the Web also. However, you will probably have to use special proprietary client software provided by the BBS company in order to access the Web. The BBS company will be able to advise you whether they provide Web access, and if so, what software is required. They will commonly be able to sell you the appropriate software, and help you should you have any problems whilst using it. They may also be able to recommend which modem you should use.

There are now thousands of BBS companies around the world. Perhaps the most well known international BBS is CompuServe. CompuServe is a long-established US-based company, which has branches globally, including the UK. There are several other major BBSs, such as Apple Computers' eWorld, specifically aimed at Macintosh users. IBM runs IBM Global Network (or Advantis), which is meant for PC users, and particularly users of IBM's own PC operating system *OS/2 Warp*. Microsoft recently launched its own BBS called The Microsoft Network, which is aimed at users of Microsoft products, such as *Windows*, and particularly *Windows 95*. Addresses for these BBS companies are also given in Appendix 3.

BBSs and other commercial Internet vendors provide phone numbers which users can dial-in to with their modems. The major Internet vendors are able to offer phone numbers in most large cities and other centres of population, and increasingly in more rural areas. The locations of these dial-in phone numbers are called PoPs (Points of Presence).

If you are going to connect to the Internet and the Web via a modem, you will be sending TCP/IP code down the phone line. There are two special versions of TCP/IP suitable for use over a

telephone line, which are known as SL/IP (Serial Line / Internet Protocol) and PPP (Point-to-Point Protocol). PPP provides error correction during transmission of data, meaning that it checks the incoming data, and if it detects an error it requests the computer sending the data to send it again. SL/IP does not provide this kind of error correction. PPP also provides better data compression than SL/IP, which means that more data may be transferred in a given time than with SL/IP, and hence it is 'quicker'. However, a drawback of PPP is that it can be tricky to install compared with SL/IP.

Commonly used SL/IP programs include *MacSLIP* and *InterSLIP* for Macintoshes, and *Trumpet Winsock* for *Windows* users. Commonly used PPP programs include *MacPPP* and *InterPPP* for Macintoshes, and NCSA *PPP* for *Windows* users.

InterSLIP is freeware, and together with *InterPPP*, produced by InterCon Systems Corporation. *MacSLIP* is a commercial program from Hyde Park Software. NCSA *PPP* is freeware. Software may normally be obtained from your Internet provider. Addresses of popular Internet providers in the UK are given in Appendix 3. TCP/IP software can also be obtained from the producers of the software. Addresses of some of the main software vendors are given in Appendix 2.

Instead of using PPP or SL/IP, some Macintosh users may be able to use ARA (Apple *Remote Access*) and a modem, to connect to a *LocalTalk* LAN, and from there to the Internet. Ultimately, TCP/IP is still used to communicate with the Internet, but the TCP/IP codes are passed back and forth, between the LAN and the remote Macintosh, via ARA. ARA acts as a conduit for the TCP/IP codes. Because ARA is involved as a 'third-party' in the process of data transmission, this means that using ARA can be slower than using PPP or SL/IP. However, ARA is commonly more stable than using PPP or SL/IP, meaning that you are less likely to lose your connection to the Internet. ARA also has the advantage that as well as using it to access the Internet, you can also use it to access and use the *LocalTalk* LAN, to which you connect with your modem. You can send documents to the LAN printer, save and retrieve files on the LAN hard disc drives, or use any other LAN facilities, such as CD-ROM drives. You can use the LAN from your Macintosh at home, just as if your Macintosh were directly connected to the LAN in the office.

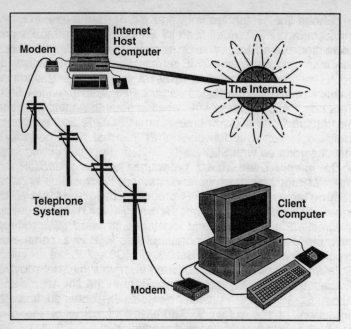

Connecting to the Internet via a modem

So there are pros and cons for each method of connecting to the Internet with a modem. Your Internet provider should be able to advise you whether PPP, SL/IP or ARA is best suited to your requirements

If your computer is connected to a LAN, which is in turn connected by a dedicated link to the Internet, then your computer is actually a permanent part of the Internet, and is said to be an Internet host computer. It will also have a host name, or IP (Internet Protocol) address, to be exact (see Chapter 2). Those who can connect to the Internet via a modem using SL/IP, PPP or ARA become temporarily connected to the Internet, and have temporary IP addresses. If you connect to the Internet via a BBS, then your computer will not be a proper part of the Internet, and will not have an IP address. Instead, the BBS computer is part of the Internet, and acts as an intermediary between your computer and the Internet.

To use the Web effectively, you will need a reasonably high performance PC or Macintosh in order to handle all the associated graphics and sound. PC users will typically need at least a 386DX computer with 4-8 MB of memory (RAM). A 'multimedia' PC is ideal for use with the Web, but you can manage without. Macintosh users will need a colour model with at least 4 MB of memory. Also, the faster the speed of your computer the better. We recommend a PC with a speed of at least 50 MHz, and a Macintosh with a speed of at least 25 MHz. PCs need to be faster since they have to run both DOS and (usually) *Windows* or *OS/2 Warp*, whereas Macintoshes need only run *System 7*. If you intend to save Web documents which include lots of graphics and sound data, you will also need plenty of hard disc space, since graphics and sound files are typically very large. For example, a photographic image downloaded from the Web will typically be several hundred kilobytes in size, whilst video and sound files are usually much larger still.

If you are going to use the Web via a modem, you should get the fastest and most reliable model that you can afford. Shop around, because some of the newer, faster models now on sale, are actually cheaper than the older, slower models which are still available. Most modems currently being sold run at either 9,600, 14,400 or 28,800 bps (bits per second), although there are still a few 2,400 bps and 4,800 bps modems around. (Note that the way modem speeds are written varies, e.g. 14,400 bps may be written 14.4 Kbps or 14K4 bps). In practice, using anything slower than a 14,400 bps modem will make using the Web frustratingly slow, since it takes so long to download and display images. Most Internet vendors can now handle modem connections at 14,400 bps, whilst a few have upgraded to 28,800 bps. Avoid using those that cannot provide at least 14,400 bps. The latest and highest standard for modems is called V34. When looking to buy a modem, look for this standard also.

Viewing Web Pages
Most statistical measures of browser usage have shown that the World's most popular browser is currently *Netscape Navigator*, from Netscape Communications. It is more commonly known simply as *Netscape*, although it is sometimes known as *Mozilla*. Versions are available for Macintoshes, and PCs running *Windows*. Its great popularity stems from the fact that it is free for

all non-commercial users, it is a very well designed piece of software which is very stable and easy to use, and all users have access to a very useful on-line help facility and manual, available at Netscape's Web site. Some other reasons for its popularity are that unlike many of its competitors, it is capable of opening several Web documents at once, and whilst it loads a Web document, it allows the user to start reading the document, and even to select a link and load another, in place of the original. This kind of flexibility is particularly important for users of modems, for whom speed of access to the Web is of prime importance. It also provides for extra facilities that other Web browsers do not, especially if the Web page being viewed has been specially set up for *Netscape*. Such pages are sometimes said to be *Netscape* enhanced, and include fancy backgrounds, highlighting devices and facilities for monetary transactions. These extra features will normally only be available if you are using the *Netscape* browser.

Throughout this book we include hints and tips for users of the *Netscape* browser. These appear in text boxes, e.g.

Netscape Hint

To 'press' one of the on-screen 'buttons' during a Netscape session, simply move the mouse pointer over the button and press the mouse button. To select a menu option in *Netscape*, move the mouse pointer over the menu item. Press and hold the mouse button, and a pull-down menu will appear. Move the mouse pointer over the menu item and proceed in this manner until you have found the menu item that you want. In this book we indicate *Netscape* menu options by giving the path from the menu bar at the top of the *Netscape* screen, e.g. Options > Preferences... indicates the Preferences option, which is found under the Options menu.

Apart from *Netscape* there are a number of other popular browsers now available for PCs and Macintoshes, which range from being freeware to fully commercial packages. The most notable are IBM *WebExplorer*, Microsoft *Internet Explorer*, and

the various versions of *Mosaic*. These browsers and several others are discussed in Chapter 8.

What does it cost?

If you can connect to the Internet at your workplace, as do many university staff and students, then you may able to access the Web at no cost to yourself. Virtually all pages on the Web are available at no charge to the user, although with some you may have to register your name and address. However, this does not mean that your usage of the Web costs nothing. The data which you transport across the Internet as you use the Web uses computer and communication resources. The costs of these are usually small enough to be met by your institution.

If you connect to the Internet via a commercial Internet provider, then you will be charged for your use of the Web. The costs will typically comprise your monthly vendor subscription costs, plus an overhead dependent on the amount of data you download. Since Web pages can be quite large (when measured in megabytes) usage of the Web can be relatively expensive compared with usage of other Internet facilities such as e-mail. Your provider should be able to advise you of their tariff for Web access, which is commonly measured in dollars or pounds per megabyte.

In addition to these costs, if you access your Internet provider via a modem, you may have to pay for the phone call whilst you are connected. It is in the interests of Internet vendors to provide as many PoPs as possible, so that most users need only make local phone calls with their modems, which means the cost of the calls will not be too high. But depending on where you live, you could have to make a long-distance call, in which case your telephone bill could become very high. Therefore it is very worthwhile choosing a vendor who can provide a local dial-in number. In some countries, such as in New Zealand and in parts of the US, local phone calls are free, which means that there are no phone charges associated with phoning a local Internet provider.

If you use a fast modem (e.g. 28,800 bps), then you will be able to download data from the Internet (and the Web) more quickly, and hence reduce the amount of time spent using the phone line. If you pay for phone calls, this can save you a lot of money in the long run, enabling you to recoup the extra cost of a fast modem, as well as making use of the Web a more

pleasurable experience. However, if you use an Internet vendor, you should check with them to see if they can handle such fast modems, and if they have a different charge rate for high speed modems. Beware some companies that actually charge a higher rate to users of high speed modems.

In general, companies which provide only Internet access are cheaper than BBS companies, simply because they provide less in the way of services, and do not have to create and manage large databases. If all you wish to do is use Internet facilities such as the Web and e-mail, the service of a basic Internet vendor company will meet your needs quite adequately, and for much less cost than a BBS.

If you would like the extra services of a BBS, make sure you shop around, comparing the costs against what you get for your money. Note that although most BBSs boast large databases of software available for downloading by their customers, a very high proportion of this same software is available free via the Internet anyway. So there is often little to be gained by going to a BBS, and less so all the time, as services once limited to BBSs are more and more often found free on the Internet, and on the Web in particular. Also, before signing-up with a BBS, check that the BBS company actually does give you easy and reasonably priced access to the Internet, including services such as the Web and e-mail. Some BBS companies prefer you to use their in-house databases and other services, and pay them for the privilege, rather than 'roaming' far and wide on the Internet and the Web, where many facilities are free. Do not let any BBS company cramp your exploration of the Internet!

The Future
The number of users of the Internet has now grown to more than 30 million worldwide, and is increasing at a rate estimated to be about 1% per day. The core of users are still university academics, government and military scientists, but the proportion of commercial and hobby users is growing very rapidly, and soon these users will predominate.

Many established users of the Internet are switching to using the Web rather than older Internet connection tools such as Telnet, FTP (File Transfer Protocol), WAIS (Wide Area Information Servers) and Gopher (see Chapter 3). Many new users of the Internet are not familiar with the older Internet tools,

since they only use the Web. This trend towards the Web as the main tool for exploring and using the Internet will continue. There are as yet no signs of a successor to the Web.

More and more commercial ventures are now waking-up to the fact that the Internet provides a potentially huge global market for their products and services. The infrastructure of the Internet is already well developed, and growing rapidly in size, as is the potential customer base. It seems that the Web provides an ideal tool for exploitation of the Internet. Until recently, it was strictly taboo to use the Internet for commercial purposes, but this principle seems to have been mostly cast aside in the rush to make money out of the Internet. Presently, the unwritten rule is that companies on the Internet must not actively advertise themselves by sending unsolicited e-mail, or by submitting advertisements to Network News, a misdemeanour termed 'spamming'. However, it is now perfectly legitimate for a company to provide its own Web server, which can be accessed voluntarily by Web users who are interested in the products or services offered by that company. The future development of the Web will probably be dominated by its increasing commercialisation.

Whilst a great deal of what is already available free on the Web will remain so, it is likely that vast amounts of new material will appear that may only be accessed after payment to the provider of that material. It may also transpire that more and more free sites which become very popular will also switch to being fully commercial. People are more likely to pay for a Web site if they have already become regular users, rather than paying for something they have never used before.

Making payments across the Web is already possible, although the technology is still in its infancy. Clearly, there are many security problems to be overcome if shopping via the Web is to become commonplace and not subject to fraud and theft. But progress on this front has been rapid and the security issues are being successfully addressed. Once buying and shopping via the Web has been established, and shown to work successfully, this will increase the trickle of companies joining the Web to a torrent.

Other developments in store for the Web will probably involve cramming ever more information into Web pages, as software and hardware technologies improve. Currently many users of the

Web use their browsers in text-only mode, i.e. they switch off all but the text component of Web pages, so that the pages download more quickly. As data compression techniques improve this will become a much less common practice. The image, video and sound components of hypermedia will become more compressed, and thus take less time to download.

Data transmission speeds will increase on Internet trunk lines and modem connections, as digital lines are increasingly used in place of analogue lines. Currently, most modem connections are made via normal, analogue phone lines. The rate at which information can be sent down an analogue line is limited by the physical properties of these lines. The maximum realistic rate is about 38,000 bps (bits per second). The introduction of digital phone networks will allow modems to operate at speeds in excess of 64,000 bps. This will also greatly reduce the time it takes to access Web pages. Digital networks are also much less prone to errors during transmission of data than analogue networks, which means that the use of digital networks will make the Web a much quicker and enjoyable tool to use.

The hypermedia aspects of the Web may also become adapted for budget, long-distance and international person-to-person communications. It is already viable to compress sound quickly and to send sound files back and forth across the Internet in real-time, between users at each end of the Internet link. Thus it is possible to use the Web as a framework for a crude, but economical phone link. The next step is to improve compression and decompression techniques and increase transmission speeds, in order to improve the quality of sound reproduction, and eventually enable the real-time transmission of video across the Internet. We can foresee the Internet being used as a means of providing personal video links across the world.

There will probably be many other developments in Web and Internet technology and new uses for both, just as unforeseeable as the eventual popularity of the Web was, when the Web was first conceived back in 1989.

Chapter 2

USING A WEB BROWSER
TO ACCESS THE WEB

Obtaining a Browser

Some of the various Web browser programs available for PCs and Macintoshes are briefly described in Chapter 8. Some of these browsers are freeware, whilst others you may have to pay for.

Many people obtain their browsers by using anonymous FTP (see Chapter 3) to download them from Internet software archives (see Chapter 4). This presupposes that you already have a connection to the Internet, and an FTP client program for your Macintosh or PC. If you obtain a browser this way, please make sure you register your copy of the software with the producers, and pay any fees that may be required.

You may also be able to get browser software from your Internet vendor, if that is how you connect to the Internet. Addresses for some of the main vendors in the UK are given in Appendix 3.

If you access the Internet via a LAN at a university or some other large institution, you can try contacting the local network administration staff, who may be able to provide you with the browser you require, or a good alternative. They may already have a site licence for a particular browser. Check to see whether the browser they offer has already been registered and paid for, if payment is required.

You can also try asking friends who use the Internet if they can let you have a copy of the browser you want. Or you may be able to get a copy from a local computer club. Make sure that copying the browser is legal. Providing it is, also make sure that you register your copy with the software producers, and pay any fees for use of the software.

If none of the above methods is suitable, you can usually place an order with the producers of the browser that you want. Postal and e-mail addresses are given in Appendix 2 for the producers of some of the most popular browsers.

It is now becoming more and more common for computers to be sold with a browser ready-installed. For example, IBM include a browser with their OS/2 Warp operating system. However, there is no reason why you should not try using other browsers instead, until you hit upon the one that you like the best.

Netscape Hint

Currently, the *Netscape Navigator* browser is free to all non-profit organisations, which covers most educational institutions and individuals. Commercial organisations must pay a licence fee. The program may be obtained directly from Netscape Communications. The company's address is given in Appendix 2. The program is also available on major Internet software archives (see Chapter 4) and also from Netscape Communications' archives (see Appendix 2), and may be downloaded using anonymous FTP (see Chapter 3).

Installing a Browser

If you obtain your browser on an installation disc, simply place the disc in your disc drive, select the installation program on the disc, and execute the program. The software will install itself, and whilst doing so, will inform you of any problems, and ask you for any information it requires. If in doubt, accept the default settings that the installation program recommends. With few exceptions, most installation programs are very well written.

If you download your browser from an Internet software archive, then the software will almost certainly be in a compressed form. You may be able to execute the compressed file, if the file is of the 'self-extracting' variety, i.e. capable of decompressing itself. Such files usually have file names ending with the extensions *.sea* (Macintosh) or *.exe* (PC). If this is not the case, you will have to use an appropriate decompression program, such as the PC program *PKZip*, or the Macintosh program *StuffIt Expander* (see the section on FTP in Chapter 3 for more information on decompressing files). The decompression program will decompress the file which you have downloaded, into one or more component files. Some of these files may be text files with

names like 'readme', or 'info'. Read these first, using a text editor program or wordprocessor program. Typically such text files can be opened and read by clicking on their icon. These text files will typically provide information on installation, and your rights to the use of the software. They may also provide information on how to use the software. When you have read these files, find and execute the installation program. As described above, the installation program should guide you smoothly through the installation procedure.

Installation of a browser will normally involve the creation of a new directory or folder on your hard disc, which is used to store the software and related files. The executable program will be stored in this folder, but you may want to create a program icon for easy access. Your *Windows* or *System 7* manuals will provide advice on how to create a program icon. Some installation programs will provide you with a program icon automatically.

Netscape Hint
The *Netscape* installer program will automatically create a Netscape directory (or folder) on your hard disc. It will place the main *Netscape* application in this directory, along with text files containing release notes, and a licence agreement. The installer will also place other important files elsewhere on your disc, and create a *Netscape* application icon for you. Simply click on the icon to start the browser.

Netscape Hint
To customise Netscape, select Options > Preferences... You can then select from a pull-down menu the Preferences you wish to change. Later in this chapter we make some suggestions.

A browser will usually need some customisation to tailor it to your requirements. This used to mean having to edit a special parameter file, typically stored in the same directory as the browser program (or on *Windows* systems, commonly in the *Windows* directory). However, most modern browsers allow you to change browser settings from within the browser program

27

itself. This facility usually appears under a pull-down menu entitled 'Preferences' or something similar.

Internet Host Names

Web pages are stored on computers around the World, each of which is connected to the Internet, and each of which has a unique name for identification on the Internet. In order for a Web browser to successfully connect to a remote Internet computer and download a Web page, it must have the correct name for the remote computer. The convention of giving Internet computers names is also essential for Internet operations other than using the Web, such as sending e-mail and transferring files using FTP. An understanding of how and why Internet computers are named is therefore fundamental to the use of the Web and the Internet.

Internet computers are often called 'Internet hosts', or some-times simply 'hosts' for short, and each has a unique IP (Internet Protocol) host name and number. The terms 'host name' and 'host address' can be used interchangeably in this context. The host names (or addresses) are constructed using a hierarchical system called the Domain Name System (DNS). The host name usually consists of 2-5 short alphabetic codes separated by full-stops ('periods' in American English), and is usually typed in lower case letters. These full-stops are commonly referred to as 'dots', so that the name *vuw.ac.nz* is said 'vuw dot ac dot nz'.

The last part of the host name is usually the country code, although this is normally omitted for hosts in the USA. For example, the host *src.doc.ic.ac.uk* has the country code *uk*. There are two-letter codes for most countries in the World. Some common ones you will come across are: *au* = Australia, *br* = Brazil, *ca* = Canada, *cz* = Czech Republic, *dk* = Denmark, *fi* = Finland, *fr* = France, *de* = Germany, *ie* = Ireland, *il* = Israel, *jp* = Japan, *nl* = The Netherlands, *nz* = New Zealand, *no* = Norway, *su* = Russia, *es* = Spain, *se* = Sweden, and *ch* = Switzerland. The country code part of the host name is also known as the 'zone'.

In the USA, the last part of the host name normally refers to the type of organisation that the host serves. For example, the host *wuarchive.wustl.edu* belongs to organisation type *edu*, short for education. This is also called the 'zone'. There are a number of other three letter zone codes that you will come across: *com* = commercial organisation, *gov* = government,

int = international organisation (mostly NATO), *mil* = military, *net* = networking organisation, *org* = any non-commercial organisation.

Outside the USA, the code to the left of the zone gives the type of organisation. For example, the host *src.doc.ic.ac.uk* belongs to organisation type *ac*, short for academic. Thus *ac* is the equivalent of *edu* in the USA. You will come across a wide variety of other codes, similar to the ones listed for the USA above, that denote the organisation type. For example, *co* means commercial, and *org* means any miscellaneous organisation.

The next code to the left of the organisation type code is usually an abbreviation of the organisation's name. For example, for the host *src.doc.ic.ac.uk*, the *ic* stands for Imperial College, which is in London. To the left again, there may be one or more codes, which refer to the particular computer that is connected to the Internet.

Network software usually uses a numerical equivalent of the IP host name called the IP host number, which comprises several integer numbers separated by full-stops. However, in general Web users should use IP host names, and not IP host numbers. Furthermore, the structure of the DNS is meant to make it easy to remember IP host names, not IP host numbers.

Uniform Resource Locators

One of the most important concepts of the Internet is that any file or other type of resource, on any Internet computer, can be specified using a URL (Uniform Resource Locator). This is a standard way of describing the name of a file, or other type of network resource, its location on the Internet, and how it may be accessed or retrieved by other Internet users. URLs are now in widespread use on the Internet, and are integral to the Web.

In general, the format of a URL is written:

method://hostname[:port]/path/filename

The 'method' is followed by the host name of the computer on which the Internet resource resides, the path to that resource, and the filename of the resource, if applicable. Optionally, a port number can be included after the hostname, which dictates the

actual port used by the computer in question. Port numbers are generally specific to different modes of Internet connection, such as Telnet, Gopher, HTTP (the Web), etc. Good Web browsers are able to handle all these URL connection methods automatically. URLs can be used to specify access 'methods' other than HTTP, and resources other than Web pages, as described in Chapter 3.

So, a typical URL for a Web page will look something like this:

URL:http://home.mcom.com/home/welcome.html

This URL is for a Web page with the file name *welcome.html*, which resides in a directory called home, on a computer with the Internet host name *home.mcom.com*. The file name extension is *.html*, which shows that the file is written in HTML, i.e. it is a Web page. This also indicates that the file may be accessed using HTTP, the standard mechanism for moving Web pages across the Internet. This is specified by *http* at the front end of the URL. Note that the code specifying the access mechanism, in this case *http*, is always followed by one colon. Also, there are never any spaces within a URL. It is important, when entering URLs into a browser, not to type in any wrong or extra characters, otherwise the URL will be invalid, and the Web resource will not be retrieved.

Commonly, the prefix 'URL:' is dropped in the interests of brevity, as will be done in this and the following chapters. So, the example given above becomes simply:

http://home.mcom.com/home/welcome.html

On some Web pages you will commonly find URLs that contain a # (hash) symbol. This does not specify another Web page, but rather another portion of the same Web page. Selecting the link will cause the other part of the Web page to be displayed. This provides a quick and easy way to move around large Web documents, rather than by scrolling the display up or down.

Other unusual characters which commonly appear in URLs include the '~' character (tilde), usually found to the left of the number 1 key on your keyboard, and the '_' character (underscore), usually found to the right of the number 0 on your keyboard, and not to be confused with the '-' character (minus or

hyphen). URLs must always be typed exactly if they are to work, including all the characters, however strange they may appear. If there are capital letters in the URL, make sure they are entered as capitals, not lower case. Also, URLs never contain any spaces.

If a URL does not work, it might be that the resource you want has been moved to another directory or the name of the resource has been changed slightly. This is very common, especially with smaller, less permanent Web sites. For this reason, although all the URLs mentioned in this book were test-ed immediately prior to going to press, it may be that one or two no longer work by the time you read this. However, the adminis-trators of a resource will usually leave a forwarding note at the old URL, which gives details of the new URL. If they have not, it may well be worth trying a shortened version of the given URL, which points only to the directory that the resource should be in. Following on from the last example, this would mean using the URL:

http://home.mcom.com/home/

This points to the directory where welcome.html resides, but would still work even if welcome.html was renamed, or some other file was there in its place. You may even be able to shorten the URL so that it simply points to the host computer, in which case the host computer will send you what it regards as its home page, or welcome page. For example:

http://home.mcom.com

If you still cannot find the Web resource you are looking for, try entering the whole name of the resource, or part of the name, into one of the 'search engines', described in Chapter 4. These special Web pages can be very useful for finding resources for which you do not have the correct URL.

URLs will be used extensively throughout this book to identify Web pages and other useful resources on the Internet. For clarity they will normally be given on a separate line and itali-cised. Always make sure you copy these URLs into your brows-er program very carefully, otherwise your browser will not be able to access the resource you want.

Netscape Hint

You can use your Netscape browser to access a URL by name. Select File > Open Location... When the Open Location dialogue box appears, enter the URL into the box. Do not start the URL reference with the letters 'URL:'. So, for a Web page, you would start by entering the characters 'http'. Make sure you have copied the URL exactly from your source, character by character. If you use a Macintosh, and you already have the URL in another document on your computer, you can copy it and then paste it into the Open Location dialogue box. Not only is copying and pasting the URL often quicker and easier than typing the URL into the dialogue box, you will also not run the risk of mistyping the URL. When you have entered the URL into the dialogue box correctly, press the 'Open' button. The URL should then be accessed by your browser, and if the URL is that of a Web page, the Web page should appear on your screen within a few seconds. A quicker alternative to the above method is to paste or type the URL into the 'Location:' panel, which lies below the button bar, near the top of the *Netscape* display. As you enter the URL, you will notice that the panel is re-labelled 'Go to:' instead of 'Location:'. This method works equally well on Macintoshes and PCs. When you have entered the URL, press the 'return' or 'enter' key.

Connection to the Web

Whichever Web browser you use, a TCP/IP connection to the Internet must be available whenever your browser program is instructed to retrieve a Web page or any other data from the Internet. If you connect to the Internet via a LAN, or some other direct connection, you will probably use *MacTCP* if you are a Macintosh user, or something like Trumpet *Winsock* if you are a *Windows* user. For modem users this will mean running software which can send TCP/IP down the phone line, using one of the protocols PPP, SL/IP or ARA (see Chapter 1).

When a browser accesses and displays a Web page, there are five key steps involved:

1. The browser opens the TCP/IP connection to the Internet host computer which holds the Web page data. The location of the Web page is specified by the user entering the Web page's URL via the keyboard, or by selecting a hypertext link that defines the URL.

2. The browser sends a request to the remote Internet host computer for the data which describes the Web page.

3. The remote Internet host computer sends the data in response. The data is received by your computer (the client computer in this operation), i.e. the data is 'downloaded'.

4. The connection between your computer (the client) and the Internet host computer is closed.

5. The browser reads the data and uses it to create a Web page display on your screen.

Your connection to the Internet must be available when the browser wants to make a connection to a remote Internet computer, and must remain available whilst any connection is open. If the Internet connection is lost for any reason, the browser will not be able to download anything. Loss of connection may cause the browser to return an error message, or may even cause the browser to 'crash'.

If your browser is not going to try and make a connection to a remote Internet computer then the Internet connection need not be available. So, in practice, if you are using a modem, this means that you may disconnect from the phone line, once a connection to a remote Internet host has been closed by your browser, without upsetting the browser program in any way. For instance, you can download a large Web document and then disconnect from the phone line before reading the document. By doing this you may save on your phone bill and connection time charges. However, you must then re-dial and reconnect to your Internet host computer, before you can download another Web document.

Netscape Hint

When making a connection to an Internet host computer, the Netscape program will show progress in a panel at the bottom of the screen display. It will show the URL of the host, when it is contacting the host, and show you when the host has been contacted. Once the download has begun, depending on which version of the software you are running, two or more figures appear in the panel at the bottom of the Netscape display. Older versions of Netscape show only the number of bytes downloaded so far, and the total to be downloaded. Newer versions show more detail: the first figure shows the percentage of that file that has been downloaded so far, followed by the total file size (in kilobytes), followed by the rate (bytes per second), followed by an estimate of how long the remainder of the download will take (in minutes and seconds). Note that when you download any given Web page, it may actually consist of several files. The above set of figures will be given for each file downloaded. Netscape also shows when downloading is finished, and the connection has been terminated. When you have downloaded a document, the current URL is shown at the top of the screen in a box labelled 'Location:'. To turn this location box on and off, select Options > Show Location.

Proxies and Firewalls

Rather than your computer connecting directly to remote Web sites, as described above, it may instead have to go via a third, intermediate computer, called a 'proxy'. For example, it is very common for LAN and WAN computers to gain access to the Web via a proxy computer, which is shared by all the users of the LAN or WAN.

Requests for Web pages are firstly sent by your browser to the proxy. If the Web page has not been accessed before, or accessed recently, the proxy will automatically connect to the remote Web site and download the required Web page. It will then automatically forward the Web page to your computer. The Web page is also stored on the proxy computer, should you request it again, or should any other users of the proxy want it in

the near future.

The advantage of using a proxy is that Web pages can be retrieved much more quickly, since they can often be retrieved from the proxy, rather than from some distant Web site. Since the data is transferred over a much shorter distance, it also means that there is less strain on Internet resources.

A 'firewall' is a special computer system, comparable to a proxy, which also sits between the Internet, and a LAN or a WAN. The firewall computer provides security and protection, so that computers 'inside' the firewall (i.e. in the LAN or WAN) are protected from users of computers 'outside' the firewall. Many companies use firewalls for their networks, which means that whilst company personnel can still access the Internet, outsiders cannot get in and access company computers. Thus the firewall assures greater protection against theft of data, and malicious damage to software and other files. If there is a firewall between your computer and the Internet, then you will have to connect to the Internet and use the Web via the firewall. You will have to set your browser so that it uses the firewall computer as a proxy. Ask your network administrators for more details.

Netscape Hint
You can specify the host names of proxies using Netscape Preferences. Select Options > Preferences... > Proxies. Enter the host names and port numbers for each type of Internet connection. If you do not know what these should be, ask your Internet provider.

Homepages
When you start your Web browser program, provided that you have a satisfactory TCP/IP connection to the Internet, it is most likely that the browser will immediately make a connection to a Web site and download a Web page. The URL of this initial Web page is a default setting stored by your browser, and is commonly the 'homepage' of the developers of your Web browser.

Almost all Web servers on the Internet provide a homepage, which is designed to be the first page that site visitors access. Homepages are meant to welcome you to the server, and be informative about what the server provides. They usually contain fancy images designed to impress, and be attractive, together with links to other important Web pages on the server. If you follow the links from the homepage to pages of lesser importance, you will generally find that the pages become less dominated by arty graphics, and more text rich.

The term 'homepage' is also used in a slightly different way, to mean the first page your Web browser loads when it is started. Most browsers allow you to set the URL of the Web page which you prefer to be your homepage. For example, you might set the homepage to be that of your company or university, or some other Web page of interest.

The Netscape Communications homepage

Buttons

Web pages allow you to do more than just select links to other pages. Provided that you have a good Web browser with graphics capabilities, you should also be able to use 'buttons'. These are exactly what you might imagine, being graphical components of a Web page that are designed to look like buttons. Often the graphics are cleverly constructed so that they look like they have some relief. To press a button, simply move the cursor over the button, by using the mouse, and then press the mouse button. Most often, buttons are really no more than links to other Web pages, but they can also be used to send information and commands to the remote computer which is providing the Web page. This is useful for any kind of interactive situation, in which you must provide responses to the Web server.

Checkboxes

As well as buttons, you will often come across 'checkboxes' which are quite similar. They provide another good way of getting some interaction from the user of the Web page. A checkbox is a graphical item on the screen which is often a small empty square, but sometimes a small empty circle. The circular variety

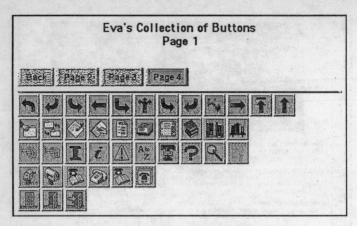

A collection of typical Web page buttons

are often called 'radio buttons'. There is commonly more than one checkbox on a Web page. Usually, some explanatory text beside a checkbox invites you to select that option. Do this by moving the cursor over the checkbox, with the mouse, and then press the mouse button. Immediately you do this, a cross will be displayed within the checkbox, or the circle will be filled with a solid circle.

Sometimes checkboxes are already 'checked' when you first download a Web page. This provides a way of giving default settings, or responses, which may be changed by the user. To 'un-check' a checkbox, simply move the cursor over the checkbox and press the mouse button. The cross or solid circle will then disappear.

When you have checked or un-checked the checkboxes on a Web page, you will normally be able to send your responses to the Web server by 'pressing' the indicated button, or selecting the indicated link. The responses are then forwarded to the Web server, which will take different actions, depending on which boxes you have checked.

Forms

A much more sophisticated method of interaction is the use of 'forms'. To use forms, you must have a Web browser with form

archive search

Check the archives you want to search:

☐ 3com-dos	☐ 3com-mac	☐ 3com-mswin
⊠ adobe-systems-any	☐ adobe-systems-mac	☐ adobe-systems-mswin
☐ alt.src	☐ aminet	☐ apple-mac
⊠ berksys-any	☐ c.s.misc	☐ c.s.unix
☐ c.s.x	☐ cd-games	⊠ cica
☐ cica-win95	☐ cica-winnt	☐ delrina-dos
☐ delrina-mac	☐ delrina-mswin	☐ delrina-mswin95
☐ epson-mac	☐ epson-mswin	☐ farallon-mac
☐ farallon-mswin	☐ farallon-mswin95	☐ garbo-pc
⊠ garbo-ux	☐ gnu	☐ hobbes-os2
☐ ibm-software-os2	☐ info-mac	☐ intel-dos
☐ intel-mswin	☐ intel-unix	☐ linux
⊠ lotus-mswin95	☐ lotus-support-mac	☐ lotus-support-mswin
☐ lotus-support-os2	☐ lotus-support-unix	☐ macromedia-mswin
⊠ macromedia-mswin95	☐ maxis-dos	☐ microsoft-softlib
☐ ms-softlib	☐ netscape-mac	☐ netscape-mswin
⊠ netscape-mswin95	⊠ netscape-unix	⊠ netwire
☐ novell-netwire	☐ oak-cpm-other	☐ pcga
☐ quest-mac	☐ quest-mswin	☐ sgigate-unix
☐ sim-msdos	☐ sim-nt	☐ sim-os2
☐ sim-ux	☐ sim-win3	☐ sim-win95
☐ tsx11	☐ umi-atari	☐ umi-mac
☐ vermeer-mswin	⊠ vermeer-mswin95	⊠ webfx-mswin
⊠ webfx-mswin95		

Checkboxes on a Web page

capability. Most do, such as Netscape, but not all. A form is a rectangular area on a Web page into which text may be entered. Forms may have a scroll-bar on the right-hand side, and/or at the bottom too. Sometimes there may be more than one form on a Web page. A form may only be large enough to enter one or two words, or may permit you to enter whole pages of text. The user can enter text into a form simply by moving the cursor into the area of the form by using the mouse, and then typing at the keyboard. The text that you type will appear within the form. Forms are not always initially empty. They sometimes contain example text, which you may edit, delete or add to. You will not be able to do any fancy formatting as you can with a wordprocessor program, since the aim is simply to get some textual response from the user. You can correct errors using the delete key, however, and you should be able to insert extra text by moving the cursor to the position of the text to be inserted. You may find that you have to press the 'return' key at the end of

every line of text, if you are to keep the text within the form area. If there is a scroll-bar to the right of the form, select the up-arrow to scroll up through the text that you have entered, or select the down-arrow to scroll down through the text. If there is a scroll-bar at the bottom of the form, use this to scroll left or right through the text.

When you have filled in the form, you will normally be able to send the text you have entered by 'pressing' the indicated button (often labelled 'submit', or something similar), selecting the indicated link, or sometimes simply by pressing 'return'. The text is then sent to the Web server computer, which will act accordingly.

Please answer all the following questions to register:

Title [Mr ▼]

First Name [ ]   Surname [ ]

Email address: [ ]

Country: [ ]
Postal Code: [ ]

Postal Address:

Sex: [Male ▼] Age: [< 10 years ▼] old.

Which best describes your occupation?

[Professional or Managerial ▼]

Which best describes the business you work in?

A typical Web page form

As an example, you may be connected to a Web server that allows you to search for some software on several Internet archives. The Web page presents you with a list of archives, and

next to each name is a check box. You are instructed to select up to six of the archives by checking six of the boxes. Once you have done this, you can enter the name of the software, by typing it into a form. To submit your request, you then press a button. The information you have entered is then sent to the Web server, which then acts upon that information. It will search the six archives, using the name that you have entered, and compile a list of possible matches. It will then send you a Web page, which shows the results of the search. The results show all the files that may possibly match your request, and in which archive they were found.

There is a wide variety of other reasons for using forms. Sometimes, forms are used as a way of sending e-mail. The text that you enter is e-mailed to the author of the Web page, or whoever is specified by the Web page. Some companies provide forms which are accessible from their homepages, which may be used to send queries, complaints, requests for information, or orders for merchandise. Authors of personal Web pages often use forms to elicit comments from readers, in order to ascertain the good and bad points of their Web pages, so that they might improve them.

Some Web pages are only accessible after you have entered your name and address into a form. This is a method of security, since the providers of the Web server will then know the identity of all the people using their Web pages. As well as a name and address, you may be asked to enter a username and password the first time you use those Web pages. Then, next time that you access those same Web pages, you will need to enter your username and password. The Web server will then check that what you have entered matches what you previously entered. The issue of security is discussed later in this chapter.

Pop-up Menus
It is also possible to include pop-up menus within Web pages, similar to those found on Macintoshes and in *Windows*. *Netscape* and most other browsers are able to display pop-up menus. Menus are a useful way of getting the reader of a Web page to make a choice from a selection of options, pre-defined by the author of the Web page.

The menu will initially appear as a box containing one line of text, including a triangular (or arrow-head) symbol at the end of

the text. To change the text currently selected within the box, simply move the cursor over the box, using the mouse, and press the mouse button. This will cause the rest of the menu to appear, as a vertical list. Simply move the mouse up or down, and release the mouse button, in order to select whichever item you want. Then, when you press the indicated button or link to submit your selection, your chosen selection is sent to the Web server.

Error Codes

Sometimes when you try to download a Web page or some other piece of data, you may instead get an error message displayed on your screen. As the design of browsers improve, more and more of these errors will be dealt with internally by the browser, and will be of no concern to the user. However, at this stage, most browsers still present some errors to the user, and these errors have associated codes, as described below.

'Bad Request 400' means that the request used the wrong syntax, i.e. it was not constructed using standard Web protocols. Check your typing of the URL before trying again.

'Forbidden 403' means that you are not authorised to receive the requested Web page or document. In this case, you may as well give up!

'Not Found 404' means that the Web server computer cannot find the item that you have requested, perhaps because it no longer exists, or it has been renamed or moved. Again, check your typing of the URL before trying again. If it really has been moved, then you may get 'Moved 301' followed by a forwarding message that includes the new URL. Follow this link to get the resource you wanted. Make a note of the new URL, and update your bookmark list if necessary. Forwarding messages are usually removed after a few weeks or months.

'Internal Error 500' indicates that the server had some problem of its own, but that you might try again later. Sometimes you will get a message to say the server is too busy, in which case you will have to be patient and try again at another time of day. 'Not Implemented 501' means that the server is not able to provide the requested facility.

If a resource has been moved or does not exist, and no forwarding message has been left to say what has happened to it, try shortening the URL as described earlier in this chapter, in

the section on URLs, so that it points only at the parent directory or the host computer. If you still cannot find the missing resource this way, try using a search engine, several of which are described in Chapter 4. If this fails, it might just be that the resource that you want simply does not exist any more.

Getting Help

As mentioned earlier in this chapter, when you first start your Web browser, it will typically load the homepage of the browser's producer, by default. All the software publishers that produce Web browsers provide Web sites for use by their customers (see Appendix 2 for URLs). Furthermore, these homepages will commonly provide links to other Web documents which provide information, hints and tips about how to use your browser. There may even be a full manual in Web format. This facility is commonly called 'on-line' help or an 'on-line' manual. Some browsers have these on-line services available from a browser menu or button, making access very easy and obvious.

Netscape Hint

To access Netscape on-line help, select Help on the top menu bar, and choose one of the options from the pull-down menu. This will download the latest help and on-line handbook pages from Netscape Communications' servers. The *Netscape* on-line handbook and other help documents are very well written and presented, with many cross-referencing hypertext links, and should answer all your queries. If you are new to *Netscape*, we highly recommend that you spend some time reading and familiarising yourself with the on-line documents.

History Lists and Caches

Most browsers offer a feature which is commonly called the 'history list' or something similar. Once you have started your browser, and downloaded a Web page, the URL of this Web page is recorded by your browser on what is called a 'history list'. If you choose a link from that first page, to another Web page,

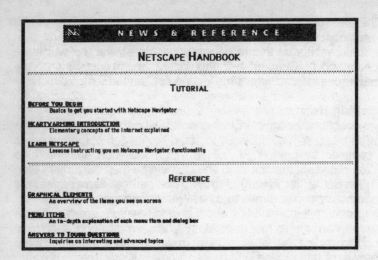

The Netscape Communications on-line handbook

the second Web page will then be added to the history list. If you move from the second page to a third page, that too will be added to the history list, and so on. This means that you can go backwards and forwards through the history list to revisit Web pages. You can go back and forth through the history list as much as you like. You can also select a URL from the history list, and so go straight to that Web page, missing out the intervening pages on the list.

However, if you return to the original Web page, and from there select a different link from the one you selected first time around, the previously created list of pages will be lost from the history list. Thus, the history list does not necessarily contain a list of all the Web sites that you have visited during one session, but rather the last 'branch' that you have followed. This feature of history lists is sometimes called 'nipping'. When you finish exploring the Web, and quit your browser, the history list is not saved. When you restart your browser, the history list will have no entries.

Related to the history list is the 'cache' (pronounced 'cash')
used by most Web browsers. The cache is computer memory or
hard disc space which is used to store the most recently downloaded Web pages, such as those that are listed on the history
list. The term 'cache' is not just used in the context of Web
browsers. It can be used to describe any portion of disc space or
computer memory reserved for storing temporary data.

If you access the Web via a proxy computer, there will be a
cache on the proxy computer, used for storing Web pages temporarily. When you access a Web page which is already stored
in the proxy's cache, you will receive that, rather than downloading the page again from the original source. The proxy cache is
used by all the Web users who connect via the proxy.

Your browser will typically set aside a portion of your computer's memory for use as a cache. When you download Web
pages, they will be stored in the cache as well as being displayed
on the screen. The memory cache is normally large enough to
hold several pages. Previously viewed pages can be quickly
retrieved by the browser from the memory cache, and redis-
played. It is much quicker to do this than to re-download Web
pages from their original sources every time they are needed.

Similarly, your browser will usually also set aside a portion of
your computer's hard disc for use as a cache. When the memory cache becomes full, the disc cache can also be used to store
Web pages. Web pages may also be retrieved by the browser
from the disc cache, which takes longer than retrieving from the
memory cache, but is still quicker than re-downloading from the
original Web source. The disc cache is usually much larger than
the memory cache, and therefore capable of storing many more
of the most recently viewed Web pages. Also, its contents are not

lost if the computer is switched off. The pages remain in the disc cache until it becomes full, in which case the oldest pages are automatically deleted. The next time these pages are requested, they will need to be re-downloaded across the Internet.

The memory and disc caches are used by the browser's history list facility. When a page is selected from the history list, it can normally be found in one of the caches, and need not be re-downloaded. Hence why the history list facility is such a quick and useful way of moving back and forth between Web pages.

The use of caches means that if a Web page is updated or changed at its source, you will not get the updated version, if there is still a copy of that page in either of your caches. This is usually not too much of a problem, because caches are limited in size, and when the caches become full, the oldest 'stale' pages are deleted. Hence, once a 'stale' page has been deleted, the next time you access the page, your browser will download a 'fresh' copy from the remote Web source. Cached Web pages are usually deleted more frequently than Web pages are changed or updated. Also, if you suspect that you have a stale version of a Web page, most browsers can be instructed to ignore the caches and re-download the page from its original Web source.

Netscape Hint
To re-download a Web page from its original source, rather than from the caches, press the 'Reload' button on the button bar at the top of the screen. This facility is also useful if you download part of a Web page, interrupt the download to do something else, but then decide that you want to see the whole Web page. Again, simply press 'Reload'.

The maximum sizes of both the disc and memory caches can usually be controlled using your browser. In theory you can increase the size of the caches until all the available disc and memory space on your computer is used, but this is not recommended! Large caches can really slow down the functioning of your computer, or even cause the computer to crash. If this appears to be occurring, use your browser to clear both caches,

and then decrease their maximum sizes to more moderate levels.

Netscape Hint
To change the size of your caches, the location of the disc cache on your hard disc, and to clear (empty) the caches, select Options > Preferences... > Cache. If you are a Macintosh user, the size of the memory cache can only be changed by entering your Macintosh's System 7 Finder, selecting the Netscape icon, selecting File > Get Info, and then altering the memory settings.

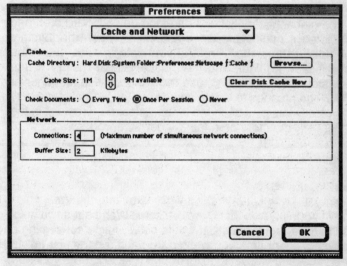

Setting your browser preferences using Netscape

With most Web browsers, as you visit various Web pages, their URLs will be appended to a file on your computer's hard disc, often called the 'global' history list. Note that only the URLs are saved, but not the actual Web pages, so the global history list file is not the same as a disc cache. The file records all the URLs

you have visited over a certain time period, which is typically the last month, although the time period may be altered. Thus, when you next start your browser, although the history list is empty of URLs, the browser still has a record of what Web pages you have previously visited. Links to these pages may be highlighted in a different colour, to indicate that they have been accessed before, at least within the last month, or whatever time period has been set. It is usually possible to open the global history list file from your browser, should you wish to select and revisit a Web page, although it is better to use the 'bookmark list' or 'hot list' facility, described in the next section. Sometimes the size of the global history file may become excessive, and use a lot of your hard disc space, in which case it may be deleted.

Netscape Hint
The global history list can be found on your hard disc, and deleted if necessary. On a Macintosh, open the 'System Folder', then the 'Preferences' folder, and then the 'Netscape f' folder, and then place 'Global History' in the wastebasket. On a PC, use the Windows File Manager or DOS commands to locate and delete the file 'netscape.hst'. Typically this may be found in the 'netscape' directory, in the 'network' directory or in the 'windows\network' directory.

Bookmarks
When you have spent a short while exploring the Web, you will almost certainly find that there are some Web pages you want to look at on a regular basis. It would be very time consuming and tedious if, every time you wanted to reach a particular favourite Web page, you firstly had to follow the links to it, from your home-page, via any number of intermediate pages. Most browsers solve this problem by allowing you to save the names and URLs of your favourite pages in a file, which is saved on your hard disc.This list, is often called the 'bookmark list', since there is an analogy with placing a bookmark in a book you are reading, so that you may quickly and easily find a particular page later on. It may also be called a 'hot list' or 'quick list', depending on which browser you happen to use.

A bookmark may be added to the list at any time whilst viewing the Web. Thereafter, you can quickly return to that page by selecting the bookmark from the full list of bookmarks. Web browsers often provide a number of ways of editing the list. The order of bookmarks may be changed, the names may be changed, and they can be grouped under appropriate headings. Sometimes it may be necessary to edit a URL too, if the location of a page changes.

Bookmarks are an extremely convenient way of getting to your favourite pages, and it is well worth investing a little time, learning how to use them, if you are to get the most from the Web. For a start, you may like to add some of the Web page URLs described in Chapters 4-8 to your bookmark list.

Netscape Hint

To add a Web page to your bookmark list, simply display the page, and then select Bookmarks > Add Bookmark. The name of the Web page will become added to the list. To retrieve that same page later, select Bookmarks, and from the pull-down menu, the name of the page. To edit the bookmark list, select Bookmarks > View Bookmarks... You then have several editing options, e.g. you can edit the name of any page on the list, or its URL. If you have several items on the bookmark list, a very useful way of organising it is to arrange the page names by categories. Each category must have its own header. The headers that you create will also appear as submenus on the Bookmarks pull-down menu. To add headers into the bookmark list, firstly click on the list to show where you want to add a new header, and then press the 'New Header' button. Enter the name of the header into the 'Name:' box. By pressing the 'up-arrow' and 'down-arrow' buttons, you can move items up and down the list until they are under appropriate headers. Also, you can hide all items under any header by double-clicking on the header. Double-clicking on a header again will make all the items under that header reappear.

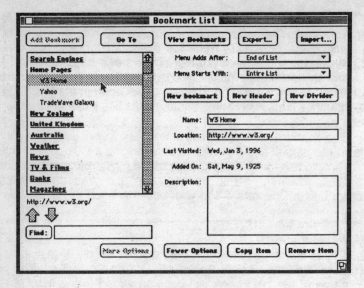

The Netscape Bookmark List

Text

Most Web pages contain both text and graphics. Very few contain text only. There are two main types of text: proportional and fixed. With a proportional font, each letter is only as wide as is necessary, so for example, an 'i' takes up less space on the page than a 'w'. Most Web pages display text in a proportional font. Fixed fonts have letters each with a fixed width, and are thus called monospaced. Fixed font text is used in tables, forms (see later this chapter) and other paragraphs which must be precisely formatted. The appearance of these text types, i.e. actual font and size, can usually be controlled by your browser program. For example, Geneva and Helvetica fonts at 10–12 point size make for easy reading. Most browsers use colour to show whether or not the text is a link or not, and if it is a link, whether that link has been selected recently. Sometimes underlining indicates a link.

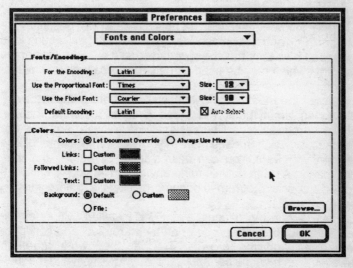

Changing text fonts and colours with Netscape

It is becoming more common to see Web pages with 'blinking' text. This is a relatively recent extension to HTML. 'Blinking' text is used merely to attract the reader's attention.

Helper Applications

All browsers can download and display text. Most can also download and display certain kinds of images, which are coded in GIF format (Graphics Interchange Format). However, to handle other kinds of images, and other kinds of files, such as sound files, video files, and compressed files, most browsers

rely on other external programs called 'helper applications'. They are so called, because they help the browser to deal with incoming data.

It is important when you start using a browser that you also acquire some helper applications, and configure your browser so that it knows which helper application to use for each file type, and where each application is located on your computer's hard disc. That way, when special files of the type described above are downloaded, the browser can start the correct helper application, and pass the file on to the helper application, which will deal with the file appropriately.

In the following sections of this chapter we describe the common PC and Macintosh file types for images, sound and video, and how they may be recognised. We also suggest some programs which may be used as helper applications in conjunction with your browser.

Many of the most commonly used helper programs are available using anonymous FTP (see Chapter 3) from Internet software archives (see Chapter 4). Most software archives are searchable, which means that if you know the name of the program you want, you can search for it by name, and then download it. As with downloading any other file, you will normally need a special program to decompress the file, before you can use it.

A few helper applications, when first installed, will automatically find your browser program on the hard disc, and configure themselves and the browser so that they work together. However, with most helper applications, you will have to manually change the settings of your browser, so that the browser knows when to use a particular helper application, and where to find it on the hard disc.

Images
Images on the Web, including graphics and photographs, are mostly coded using one of two different binary file formats, named GIF and JPEG (Joint Photographic Experts Group). GIF images are sharper, with saturated colours, and are typically used to construct logos, icons, buttons and similar graphical components within Web pages. GIF files can hold images with up to 256 distinct colours, from a palette of about 16 million.

Once you have installed your helper applications on your hard disc, you will need to tell *Netscape* when to use them, and where on the hard disc they are. To do this, select Options > Preferences... > Helper Applications. A scrolling menu lists file types and corresponding helper applications, if any have already been chosen. Click on the line which contains the file types for which you wish to configure a helper application. Click the Browse button to select an appropriate helper application to use. Press the radio button for Launch Application followed by OK. Alternatively, you can use the browser to view some file types, such as GIF and JPEG, in which case you do not need to select a helper application, and instead simply press the radio button for 'Use Browser as Viewer'. For file types that cannot be handled by the browser, or any of your helper applications, you should press the buttons for either 'Unknown: Prompt User', or 'Save'. The latter choice will cause files of the type specified to be saved to disc. You can specify the location where such files are to be saved by selecting Options > Preferences... > Directories. Use the Browse button to choose the directory, into which files will be placed. At any time whilst browsing the Web, you can save any Web resource as a file on your hard disc. To do this, when using the mouse to select the link to the item, also press either the 'option' key if you have a Macintosh, or the 'shift' key if you have a PC. The Web resource you have selected, whether it is a Web page, an image or whatever, will be downloaded to disc. You will be prompted for a file name and location.

JPEG is more suited for realistic images such as scanned photographs, with up to 16.7 million colours per picture (in theory). The main disadvantage of JPEG is that JPEG files are bigger than GIF files. In practice, you will of course be limited by the capabilities of your colour monitor, as well as the software you use to display the GIF and JPEG images.

Virtually all browsers are capable of downloading and decoding GIF images automatically, and displaying them on the screen

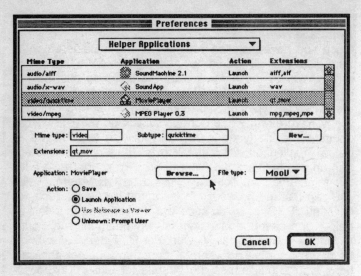

Configuring helper applications for use with Netscape

in their correct location, together with the text. An image displayed as part of a Web page is said to be 'in-line'. Some in-line images are called 'thumbnail' images. A thumbnail image is usually a small image linked to a larger version of the same image, which may be downloaded if required, and saved as a file on your disc drive.

Some browsers can handle in-line JPEG images, but if yours does not, you will need to use a separate application to download and display these images. Even so, you may wish to download, display, edit and save GIF and JPEG images as separate files. Popular programs which allow you to do this include *WinGIF*, *LVIEW*, and *JPEGView* for *Windows* users, and *GIFConverter* for Macintosh users.

Netscape Hint

The Netscape browser has an in-built capability to download and display JPEG images as in-line images. Select Options > Preferences... > Helper Applications > image/jpeg. Press the radio button for 'Use Browser as Viewer'.

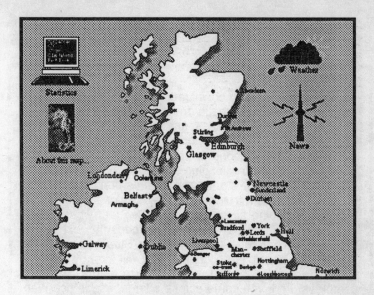

A 'clickable' image map, which is a map of the UK

Graphic and picture images are not just used for illustration, and decoration of Web pages. Some images are also links, which may be selected, as you would a highlighted text link. Some images are used to provide more than one link, and are sometimes called 'image maps'. The desired link can be chosen by selecting the appropriate part of the image map. For example, the image map may truly be that of a map of, say, the UK. Selecting the symbol on the image map marking the location of London may lead you to a Web page about London, and selecting a symbol marking Edinburgh may lead you to a page about Edinburgh, and so on.

More commonly, the image map may show several panels of text and/or pictures, which lead to various Web resources.

Downloading and displaying graphic and picture images can be time consuming, so many Web users set their browsers to download and display only the text component of Web pages. If you are in a hurry, or you have a particularly slow computer or slow connection to the Internet (such as via a slow modem) then it may be a good idea to switch off image-downloading by setting your browser's preferences. If you come across a page that you

would like to see the images on, you can always instruct the browser to re-download the page including images.

Netscape Hint

To stop images being downloaded, select Options > Auto Load Images. To turn image downloading back on, reselect Options > Auto Load Images, and so on. If you wish to keep your preferred setting for future *Netscape* sessions, select Options > Save Options. If you have just downloaded a page with image downloading turned off, but would like to see it with the images, press the 'Images' button on the button bar. *Netscape* will respond by re-downloading the page, this time including all images. Note also that when downloading a Web page, *Netscape* downloads the text before the images. Therefore, if you press the 'Stop' button, as the images are beginning to appear, you will already have all the text downloaded, and will be able to read it. This is a useful feature if you come across a large, image-rich Web page, which is taking too long to download, when all you really want to do is to read the associated text.

Some Web servers also provide specially designed pages which are text-only, as an alternative to the pages with both text and images. These pages download in significantly less time. They may be less attractive to look at, but are usually functionally identical to their counterparts which include images.

However, in general, by viewing text only, you do miss out on a lot of the more attractive and useful features of the Web. The time it takes to download and display Web pages can be improved dramatically by using a well designed and efficient browser, a fast computer with plenty of memory, and, if you use a modem, using the fastest one you can afford. Some browsers download and display text first, and the graphical elements second, so that you can carry on reading the text, whilst the rest of the page downloads. This useful facility helps to save time. Some Web pages contain interlaced GIF images, which first appear with low resolution and then improve until the entire image has arrived, as opposed to arriving a line at a time, from the top row to the bottom. This means you can get a quick idea

of what the entire image will look like while waiting for the rest. However, some browsers do not support progressive display as the image is downloaded, in which case the image will not be displayed until it has arrived in its entirety.

Netscape Hint
The *Netscape* browser supports interlaced images, so the images should gradually appear as they are downloaded. If not, select Options > Preferences > Images. Press the radio button marked 'While Loading'.

Although GIF and JPEG have become the most commonly used graphics formats on the Web, there is every possibility that with time they will become superseded by other formats. Improvements are possible in terms of increasing the compression, and hence decreasing the size of files, and in improving the clarity of images and colour rendition.

Sound

Another feature of the Web is the availability of sound, or audio files. These can be downloaded like any other resource, by selecting the appropriate Web link. Most browsers rely on using a helper application to play sound files, but these applications are widely available as freeware or shareware for PCs and Macintoshes. Your computer must also have the appropriate hardware in order to be able to produce sound.

There is a wide variety of sound file formats. The sound format of any given file may normally be deduced by looking at the file name extension, i.e. the letters after the full-stop. The common sound formats have the file name extensions *.aiff, .aif, .au, .iff, .mid, .ra, .snd, .voc* and *.wav.* Depending on which audio player program you use, you will be able to play one or more of these sound formats.

All modern Macintoshes can play audio, without the need to purchase extra hardware, and some models even have built-in stereo sound. *Sound Manager* is Apple Computer's program for playing and recording sounds on a Macintosh or Power Macintosh, specifically *.au* files. The program comes with System 7, and can be controlled using a special Control Panel.

The latest version can be downloaded from Apple's anonymous FTP and Web sites, as well as other sites.

Other popular audio programs include *SoundApp* and *Sound Machine*. *SoundApp* is a freeware Macintosh program, capable of playing a large variety of formats, including *.au* , *.aiff*, *.snd*, *.wav*, and *.voc* files. Files need only be dropped onto the *SoundApp* icon to be played or converted between formats. *Sound Machine* is a popular freeware Macintosh program, capable of playing *.snd*, *.au* and *.aiff* files. It is ideal for use as a Web browser helper application, and offers a good selection of facilities.

Nearly all PCs have an internal loudspeaker of some kind, which may be used to play some sound files. To do this, you must firstly install a PC speaker driver program. The driver may not produce high quality sound on all computer systems and may often be rather quiet. The performance of the driver largely depends upon the make and model of your PC. However, at least you can hear the sound. A popular driver for *Windows* is a piece of software called *speak.exe*, written by Microsoft and available as freeware from anonymous FTP archives.

Many modern PCs, often called 'multimedia' PCs, come complete with built-in sound-cards and high quality speakers, either internal or external to the computer. A multimedia PC is ideal for use with the Web. If you do not have a multimedia PC, and only have a standard internal speaker, you can upgrade your computer by installing a sound-card and external speakers. Sound systems are available from a variety of manufacturers of PC hardware. A very popular and widely supported sound system for PCs is called *SoundBlaster*.

For MIDI (Music Instrument Digital Interface) files (*.mid* file extension) you will definitely need a specialised music synthe-siser sound card in your computer. There are several programs around dedicated to MIDI files. One such shareware program is *Music Sculptor* by Aleph Omega Software. It works with any synthesiser and sound card compatible with *Windows*. The hard-ware demands of other sound file types are not so demanding as MIDI.

The Microsoft *Windows* standard sound format is *.wav*, and the Microsoft *Windows* application *Mplayer* is capable of playing these files. There are others too, such as *Digital Audio Playback Facility*. This application is a shareware program for *Windows*.

It can play *.wav* and *.mid* files. The latter depends on you having the appropriate synthesiser card installed. *GoldWave* is another shareware program for *Windows* and requires a sound card. It can load, play and edit many different sound file formats, such as *.wav*, *.au*, *.voc*, and *.snd* files.

Wham is a widely used freeware *Windows* program, recommended for use with *Mosaic* and *Netscape* Web browsers. *Wham* (Waveform Hold and Modify) can read and write *.wav* files, and files of several other formats including *.snd*. *Wham* can handle sounds of any size, restricted only by memory.

Winplany is a very simple, but effective *Windows* sound player, which supports *.voc*, *.au*, *.wav*, *.snd*, and *.iff*, and files of any size, only limited by available memory. It works well with the PC speaker driver. *Winplany* is also a recommended helper application for *Mosaic* and *Netscape*.

If you do not want to use a *Windows* application, *Scoptrax* is shareware for DOS. It can play *.voc*, *.iff* and *.snd* files with or without a sound card, on 286, 386 and 486 PCs.

With all sound formats except *.ra*, when a hypertext link to an sound file is selected, the file is first downloaded, before it is passed on to the audio player application, and played. Since sound files are often very large, it can take some while to download them. In general, be prepared to wait longer than you would when downloading an image. Also, it is not possible to start listening to a sound until the file has downloaded in its entirety. When a sound file is played, you may have to adjust the controls of the audio player program, so that the sound is played at the right speed, for proper reproduction. Most sound programs allow you to go forward and reverse through a sound file, as if you were playing an audio tape on a tape player. They commonly also provide 'fast-forward' and 'fast re-wind' facilities.

However, *.ra* files may be downloaded and played simultaneously, using a freeware player from RealAudio. Versions for both Macintoshes and *Windows* are available from RealAudio's Web site. Since the sound is reproduced in real time, quality suffers, depending on how fast your modem is (if you use a modem), the speed of your Internet link and the speed of your computer.

Video

There are three common file formats for storing video, which may
be recognised by the file name extensions *.mpeg*, *.avi* and *.mov*.
These formats are, respectively, Motion Picture Expert Group
(MPEG) format, Microsoft *Video for Windows*, and Apple
QuickTime. MPEG files also sometimes have the extension *.mpe*
or *.mpg*. There are only a few commonly used video player programs for PCs and Macintoshes, since the medium is still at a
rather early stage of development.

MPEGplay is a popular shareware *Windows* program for
.mpeg video files. This program is ideal for use as a Web helper
application. The program has a number of facilities for controlling
the playing of the video clip. Note that until you register this
program, it is only able to load files up to 1 MB in size, which is
not particularly big for a video file.

If you have Microsoft's *Windows Media Player*, then there are
freeware extension programs available from Internet software
archives, which allow both *.mpeg* files and *.mov* (QuickTime)
movies to be played using this software. For *.avi* files you will
need to use the commercial *Video for Windows* program, available from Microsoft.

If you are a Macintosh user, Apple Computer's *MoviePlayer*
application will play *.mov* (QuickTime) files. *Sparkle*, is a full-
featured freeware player, and can handle both *.mov* and *.mpeg*
files. This is a recommended helper program for use with
Macintosh Web browsers.

Video files are generally even bigger than sound files, and
hence can be tediously slow to download. Also, most files available on the Internet typically only provide a few seconds worth of
moving images, small image areas, and may not always include
sound. So do not expect full length movies! For example, a typical 30 second QuickTime movie file will occupy about 2 MB, and
will take about 30 minutes to download across the Internet using

a fast (28,800 bps) modem. Unless you have a very fast PC or Macintosh, running only your video player program and nothing else, video clips will often play so slowly that you can easily see the video frames being updated. Clearly the speed of downloading and the speed of playback are currently somewhat unsatisfactory. Hopefully, as video compression techniques improve, it will become possible to download smaller files that contain longer video sequences. In addition, as computers become faster, playback speeds will become more acceptable.

Commerce on the Web

One of the most hyped features of the Web is the ability to order and buy products and services via the Internet. The reality is that at present, the opportunities for shopping via the Web in the UK are still somewhat less than in the USA, and some other parts of the world. However, the number of UK sites offering services and products via the Web, is increasing all the time, and quite rapidly too (see Chapter 5).

The Web promises much for those hoping to sell via the Internet, since there are already millions of Web users worldwide. The size of the revenue which could be generated by such a huge potential customer base has already attracted a large number of companies to set up shop on the Web. Also, the commercial sector perceives Web users to be relatively affluent and thus ideal customers!

Many companies now use Web sites to advertise their products and services to a world wide audience. Setting-up a Web server requires very little investment of time or money, compared to conventional advertising, and can reach a global audience. For companies that do not have enough expertise of their own to set up a Web server, there are already Internet companies that provide Web advertising services. In the UK, companies such as Atlas, CityScape, Demon, EUnet, Unipalm-PIPEX and RedNet offer services for organisations interested in getting started on the Web.

A company Web site will typically provide an attractively designed company homepage, with the company logo, and links to other Web pages which describe what the company has to offer. These Web pages will typically include catalogues of items for sale, sales information, information and history of the company, details of after-sales service, and perhaps links to other

61

affiliated companies and sites of interest. It is clearly very important that the pages be attractively presented, informative and even entertaining, otherwise potential customers will quickly leave to explore other pages of the Web. Often, companies provide lists of retail outlets on their Web pages, which the user may visit, if in a convenient location; while other commercial users provide postal addresses, fax numbers or e-mail addresses, for customers to place their orders. Goods may be sent to the customer by courier or mail.

A problem facing any business trading on the Web is how to entice Web users to access the company homepage. One answer to this problem is to advertise via the Web. Advertisements are now appearing more and more commonly on all types of Web pages. A few parts of the Internet remain somewhat anti-commercial, such as Network News. Advertising via Network News is called 'spamming' by the users. However, even attitudes on Network News are changing. Limited advertising is now acceptable on some newsgroups, such as *alt.business* or *misc.entrepreneur* (see Chapter 3 for more information on Network News).

Addressing the needs of commerce on the Internet, there are a growing number of commercial Web sites that provide a showcase for businesses which wish to advertise, provide services and products via the Web. In their simplest form, such Web sites may offer a searchable list of businesses, or list businesses under various categories. For each business, there may simply be a company resume, or there may be a link to the company homepage, with details of products and services on offer.

More often now, these 'umbrella' sites for companies developing business on the Internet, are styled as 'virtual shopping malls'. A 'virtual shopping mall' typically comprises one or more Web pages that provide a graphical representation of a typical shopping mall. Simply by pointing and 'clicking' with the mouse on the graphical representation of a business, you can 'enter' the business, browse through the available products and services, and place your order.

Web sites that host more than one business are rapidly becoming popular, as evidenced by the appearance of well known high-street shops, banks and brand names on these sites. Many people now turn to the Web when they want

something, in the same way that they used to turn to the Yellow Pages.

Security
Until relatively recently, a major obstacle to commerce on the Internet was lack of security. Data sent via the Internet is generally not very secure, since it takes a circuitous route through several intermediary computers to reach any destination computer. The actual route your data takes is not under your control, and at any intermediate location on its journey to or from your computer, there is a possibility that it may be read, copied, altered, or destroyed. So for example, if you send your credit card details across the Internet, the information could be intercepted by some unauthorised person, and used fraudulently. There are many hackers competent enough to develop a system which monitors Internet traffic, and looks for tell-tale character strings such as 'Visa', 'MasterCard' or long numbers that begin with a 4 for Visa, or a 5 for MasterCard.

To prevent this from happening, new methods are being developed that allow secure financial transactions to be made via the Internet. Some of these methods are described in this section, although there are new ones appearing all the time. As Internet security increases, shopping and making payments via the Web will become easier and less risky.

Financial transactions are just one example of how security on the Internet and the Web is an important issue. There are also many other instances when information exchanges across the Internet should be completely private. For example, they might involve technological, business, or military secrets, or they might be politically sensitive.

Transfer of confidential information across networks such as the Internet (including the Web), is usually done with the use of programs which are able to code and later decode the information. The science of coding and decoding is called cryptography. The process of creating a coded message is called encryption. There are many encryption methods, but perhaps the most commonly used one on the Internet is called RSA. RSA is a system for both encryption and authentication, invented in 1977 by Ron Rivest, Adi Shamir, and Leonard Adleman. The name 'RSA' is an acronym, being the initials of the inventors' surnames. RSA has since been patented, and is now marketed by RSA Data

Security, Inc.

RSA is a good example of a 'public-key' encryption system. When you start using an RSA program, the program generates two 'keys' that belong uniquely to you. These are not physical keys, such as the keys in your pocket, but you may think of them as digital analogues. One key is secret, is usually called the private key, and stays in your computer. The other key is called the public key. This second key is transmitted via the network to other computers with which you exchange data. The public key allows other computers to transmit data in an encrypted form to your computer, but the data can only be unencrypted using the private key, stored on your computer. Thus, to send secure data across a network you only need the recipient's public key, but to decode secure data, you need both keys.

One of the most popular implementations of RSA on the Internet is a system known as SSL (Secure Sockets Layer). SSL provides a 'layer' of security between TCP/IP and the standard internet protocols, such as HTTP (i.e. the Web), FTP (file transfer), SMTP (i.e. e-mail), NNTP (i.e. Network News), Telnet, and Gopher (see Chapter 3 for more details). It also provides server authentication, which means that users cannot pretend to be who they are not, and encryption, meaning that anyone who eavesdrops on an SSL communication cannot understand what has been transmitted. Finally, it protects data integrity, meaning that the data cannot be altered by any unauthorised person. Web servers that provide SSL security can easily be recognised, since they have URLs starting with *https:* rather than the normal *http:*. Similarly, a Network News server offering SSL would have a URL starting with *snews:* rather than the usual *news:*, and so on.

Microsoft and Visa International recently announced a new RSA-based technology for secure financial transactions on the Internet. The system is known as Secure Transaction Technology (STT), and is completely integrated with the current bank card system. Microsoft and Visa have made the specification freely available in order to encourage the development of STT-compliant applications. Microsoft's *Internet Explorer* Web browser is one of the first to use the new STT standard.

Netscape Communications use SSL, but have recently announced a system called *Secure Courier*, which is compatible with SSL, but offers even better security, and will soon be

compliant with STT. The system works by encrypting a consumer's financial information all the way from the consumer's PC or Macintosh to the financial institution. In addition, *Secure Courier* enables consumer authentication for vendors. Whilst SSL encrypts data passing along a network between a client and a server computer, *Secure Courier* keeps the financial data encrypted, in a 'secure digital envelope', when it arrives at a vendor's server or at other intermediate points on the network. The data remains 'wrapped' or protected at any site at which it stops. Like other products from Netscape Communications, *Secure Courier* is free for non-commercial use and available for a fee to commercial users.

Another popular network system which uses RSA is called PGP (Pretty Good Privacy). PGP also employs an encryption system called IDEA, created in 1990 by Xuejia Lai and James Massey. Shareware and freeware PGP programs are available for both PCs and Macintoshes from a number of software archives. However, there are several versions available, not all of which are compatible. Also, some versions are restricted by law to the USA, and hence should not be used in the UK. Another similar program to PGP, which uses RSA, is called PEM. Like PGP, some versions of PEM may not be exported from the USA, even via the Internet. Some Web browser programs can use PGP and PEM, such as NCSA *Mosaic*.

There is now also a completely new network security system called 'Shen'. Shen is being developed by Phillip M. Hallam-Baker of CERN, specifically for use on the Web. However, at the time of writing, there are as yet no implementations of Shen for PCs or Macintoshes.

RSA encryption is used by a variety of new companies which offer secure Internet financial transaction services. Companies such as DigiCash and CyberCash offer users the ability to make secure 'electronic cash' and credit card payments via the Internet (see Chapter 5 for more on these companies). It is likely that companies such as these will eventually all adhere to the Internet security standards being developed by the major established international banks, and credit card agencies such as MasterCard and Visa.

Chapter 3

USING A WEB BROWSER
FOR OTHER INTERNET ACTIVITIES

Network News
Network News, or 'Net News' for short, is a world wide conferencing system also known as 'Usenet', short for 'users' network'. Network News may be transmitted via the Internet using NNTP (Network News Transfer Protocol). Most users of the Internet are able to access Network News. Furthermore, some Network News items may also be reached via the Web, and some Web browsers provide the user with the ability to read and contribute to Network News.

Since Network News is not owned by any person or organisation, it is largely unregulated and uncensored. It is run by volunteers around the world, and is supported by the millions of users of the Internet and other networks. Furthermore, Network News is absolutely free, although you will still have to pay any Internet access fees, if you normally have to do so.

The Network News system allows users to enter messages that may then be read by thousands or even millions of other users, either within their local geographic area, within their country, or all around the world. Messages are always sent, or 'submitted' to a 'newsgroup', which has a special name and a common theme, e.g. sport, science, TV shows, cars, etc. Messages sent to newsgroups are usually called 'articles', and the process of placing an article in a newsgroup is called 'posting'. Users can also respond to any messages if they wish, either by sending a 'follow-up' message, or by sending e-mail to the original sender. A succession of 'follow-up' articles, all on the same subject, is called a 'thread'.

Some newsgroups are 'moderated' by a volunteer, usually the person who set up the newsgroup in the first place. Such a person is called the 'moderator'. When an article is submitted to a moderated newsgroup, it is firstly checked by the moderator, who will then post the article, providing it is appropriate to the newsgroup, it is reasonably interesting, and does not break any

of the standards or rules of the newsgroup. Sometimes moderators may see fit to edit long articles, or articles that may be offensive. Clearly this is a form of censorship, but in practice this means that the quality of the articles is generally higher than in unmoderated groups. Also, there are plenty of unmoderated newsgroups for those who dislike the idea of any kind of censorship.

There are now more than 5,000 newsgroups (and increasing rapidly all the time), and it has been estimated that more than 30,000 articles are posted every day, so it is important to be reasonably selective about which newsgroups you wish to subscribe to, and read on a regular basis.

Newsgroups are arranged and named using a hierarchical system. The most important top-level hierarchies are called *alt, comp, misc, news, rec, sci, soc*, and *talk*. These cover a huge variety of topics, as described below:

alt   An unofficial hierarchy of 'alternative' newsgroups, that covers a vast range of topics which are generally not covered in the official hierarchies. The newsgroups in this hierarchy tend to appear and disappear quite quickly.

comp   Covers all discussion of computer related topics.

misc   Covers a miscellany of topics.

news   Provides news and information about Network News itself.

rec   Covers all types of recreational activities, such as sports, games, arts, etc.

soc   These are a collection of social groups, where discussion can take place between people with mutual social interests.

talk   Mainly for debates and discussion. These groups tend to be rather political in content.

Newsgroups within these categories are available to nearly all Internet newsgroup sites world wide, although few Internet sites

carry a large number of the 'alt' newsgroups. Also, within your country, town or institution, there are often newsgroups which are only of local interest. For example, at Edinburgh University, there is a hierarchy called *eduni*, which carries articles concerning that university.

Newsgroups are named depending on their position within a newsgroup hierarchy. For example, there are two newsgroups, whose full names are *rec.games.bridge* and *rec.games.chess*. Both of these newsgroups belong to the games sub-hierarchy of the *rec* hierarchy. There are other newsgroups within *rec*, however, such as *rec.food.veg*, for example. Some newsgroup names can be very long, if they are near the bottom of a hierarchy, e.g. *comp.sys.ibm.pc.hardware.storage*. Newsgroups with long names tend to be of specialist interest. The parts of the newsgroup name are always separated by full-stops.

Look out for the abbreviation *.d*, which stands for 'discussion'. For example, *rec.humor* is a newsgroup for those who want to post and read jokes, whereas *rec.humor.d* is a newsgroup for those who want to discuss humour. There is a subtle difference that should be observed by posters of articles, if they are not to be rebuked by other Network News readers.

If you are new to Network News, and have never posted an article before, you may like to send a test article to one of the .test newsgroups, to see if your system is working. When you post such an article, you may get e-mail messages sent to you automatically by remote network computers, telling you that your test article has been received. Once you are satisfied that you know how to post articles, you can then compose a proper article and submit it to the relevant newsgroup.

Sometimes it is easy to guess what a newsgroup may be about, just by looking at its name. However, some newsgroup names are a little confusing, misleading or virtually meaningless, particularly within the *alt* hierarchy. The best way to find out what a newsgroup is about is to subscribe to it and read the articles that have been posted. It is always possible to unsubscribe later, if the topics discussed in the newsgroup are not of interest.

Articles posted to a newsgroup do not stay there for ever, otherwise Network News would have become terminally congested many years ago! Many articles are set to time-out when they are posted, i.e. they are marked so they will be deleted after a specified time. Sites where Network News is received

automatically are known as 'newsfeeds'. System administrators in charge of newsfeeds may delete all articles that are more than a few weeks old, simply to conserve hard disc storage space. Articles in some newsgroups may last longer than others, depending on how much usage those newsgroups get. Usually, news feeds only carry a limited selection of newsgroups, including ones of local and international interest. The administrator at each site usually has arbitrary and total control over which newsgroups are carried, but is generally open to suggestions. Site news administrators provide one of the main forms of control and censorship of Network News.

To be able to read Network News, you should be connected to the Internet in the same manner you normally connect to use the Web. Also, it is essential that you should have access to a newsfeed, i.e. a local computer on the Internet which will accept and retrieve newsgroup articles for you. Most universities and other large institutions provide newsfeeds. If in doubt, ask your Internet provider.

Given access to an Internet newsfeed, you may access Network News from your Macintosh or PC with a program known as a 'newsreader'. There are a number of dedicated newsreader programs around for both PCs and Macintoshes, most of which are shareware or freeware, and available for downloading from major anonymous FTP sites and Web archives. Newsreader programs for Macintosh computers include *Internews*, *Newshopper*, *Nuntius*, *Newswatcher* and *TheNews*. Popular newsreader programs for PCs include *Free Agent*, *News Xpress*, *Trumpet Newsreader* and *WinVN*. Some Web browsers have newsreader capabilities already built-in. Alternatively, your browser may be able to start-up an independent newsreader application, when it is required.

Netscape Hint
To access Network News with Netscape, you must tell your Netscape program the location of your newsfeed. Select Options > Preferences > News. Enter the name of your newsfeed into the box labelled News (NNTP) Server.

Before attempting to read Network News, you must enter into your newsreader program, or your browser, the Internet address of your newsfeed computer, otherwise the program will not know where to look for news articles.

You will commonly see newsgroups given as hypertext links on Web pages. Selecting such a link should start your browser's newsreader facility, if it has one, or cause your browser to start up your favourite newsreader program. These newsgroup links are actually URLs with the format *news:newsgroup*, for example:

news:alt.peeves

The URL specifies the name of a newsgroup, in this case *alt.peeves*. Remember that news feeds never carry a full selection of all the Network News groups that exist world wide, so it is entirely possible that you may not always be able to access URLs mentioned on Web pages.

A newsreader will typically allow you to subscribe to any number of the newsgroups that are available from your local newsfeed. These will normally be a mix of international newsgroups on subjects of interest to you, and local newsgroups.

A list of subscribed newsgroups (using the Netscape newsreader)

71

By selecting a newsgroup with your newsreader, you can read the latest articles. Each article has a title and an author. Articles are normally arranged in threads. All replies to one original article will be in one thread, so each thread normally covers a different topic. In a list of newsgroup articles, different threads are usually indented so that they may be distinguished easily.

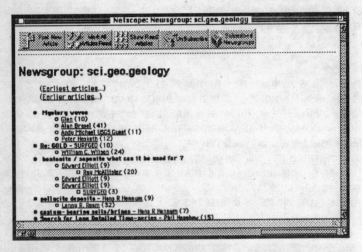

A list of articles in a newsgroup (using the Netscape newsreader)

When you read an article, you will notice that at the top of the article is a header, containing not only the title of the article, but the name of the author, the author's organisation or affiliation (e.g. company name, university name, etc.), and the author's e-mail address. Also, there is a list of the names of the other newsgroups to which the article has been sent, if any. Beneath the header is the article itself, which is typically only a paragraph or two in length, but may be longer. Articles normally finish with the authors 'signature', which comprises the name of the author, address, phone number and other contact details.

Articles contain only text, since NNTP cannot handle images or other multimedia. However, sometimes you will see articles in which text is used to encode non-textual files, such as image and sound binary files. The most common codes used in Network News are BinHex and UUencode. You will need a special

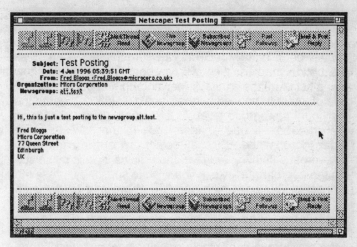

Reading a Network News article (using the Netscape newsreader)

program to decode such articles, and from them reproduce the original binary file. Your newsreader program may already have a built-in facility for doing this. Otherwise BinHex coded files may be decoded on a Macintosh using such programs as _BinHex_, _StuffIt Expander_ or _Compact Pro_, and on a PC using _WinCode_. UUencoded files may be decoded on a Macintosh using _DropStuff with Expander Enhancer_, and on a PC using _WinCode_ (for more information on file decoding and decompression, see the section on FTP later in this chapter).

A newsreader will normally also have a basic text editor facility, which will allow you to type an article of your own. Your article may follow-up other articles in a thread, or may be the start of a new thread. Once you have typed your article, it may be submitted to the newsgroup, or even a number of different newsgroups, for other users to read. Some newsreaders also allow you to respond to an article by sending e-mail to the author, rather than by submitting a follow-up article to the newsgroup.

When writing articles for Network News, there are some basic 'rules' of net etiquette ('netiquette'). Firstly, when beginning an article, formal salutations are virtually unknown, and salutations of any kind are barely necessary at all. Always make sure your contributions are relevant to the newsgroups to which you send them. There is nothing more annoying for readers of newsgroups

Netscape Hint

If you would like to see what newsgroups are available to you, select Directory > Go to Newsgroups, and then press the button marked 'View All Newsgroups'. This will show you a list of all the available newsgroup hierarchies. Select one of interest, and keep selecting links until you get to the individual newsgroup level. At this stage, you may click on the checkbox, if one appears next to the newsgroup, in order to subscribe. You may select any of the highlighted newsgroups shown, and read the articles therein by selecting the appropriate links. If you wish to subscribe, press the 'Subscribe' button, which appears above and below each article. Alternatively, select Directory > Go to Newsgroups, and enter the name of the newsgroup you wish to subscribe to, into the dialogue box. The browser will then check to see if the newsgroup is available on your local newsfeed. If the newsgroup you select is available on your local newsfeed, it will add it to the list of subscribed newsgroups. Later, if you wish to unsubscribe to any newsgroup, check the box next to the newsgroup on the list, and press the Unsubscribe button. To read articles, click on a highlighted link to a newsgroup. This will cause all currently available articles to be loaded, sorted and displayed. Articles in a thread are indented below the initial article. To read an article, click on the link to the article. There are buttons above and below the newsgroup and article displays which give you a variety of options, e.g. set all articles as read (mark all articles read); return from an article to the corresponding newsgroup; return to the list of subscribed newsgroups; post a new article; post a follow-up article; and, reply by e-mail to the poster of an article. The article posting and e-mail facilities will produce a form on your screen, for you to fill in and send. You may also follow links from Web pages to newsgroups, provided the specified newsgroups are held on your particular newsfeed (if not, you will get an error message). If you do so, you may then select the 'Subscribe' option from the button bar at the top of the newsgroup article list.

than having to wade through masses of irrelevant postings. If in doubt, read the FAQ (Frequently Asked Questions) documents, which are regularly posted to most newsgroups. These documents will tell you all about the newsgroup, its functions, its rules, and answer many of the queries you may have. Whenever possible, check the FAQ before you submit a question to the newsgroup. If you cannot find any FAQs immediately, wait for a few days and one will almost undoubtedly be posted by one of the newsgroup regulars. Alternatively, you can post a request for the FAQ. If in doubt, 'lurk' for a while, reading the contributions from the regulars and old-timers, before diving in yourself.

Try to keep your postings well written, and concentrate on being as concise as possible. Good spelling and grammar are important. You may not feel that these qualities should be important in what is basically a very informal medium, but it makes your posting much easier for other people to read and understand. Furthermore, people are more likely to read your posting than skip over it, or give up half way through. An eloquent piece is much more interesting to read, and much more persuasive.

Make sure that the line length setting of your text editor or word-processor program is not too long, and definitely not more than 80 characters, since display windows are rarely wider than 80 columns. Otherwise, your lines may wrap-around making your article very difficult and confusing for other people to read. You can always make your lines shorter by adding extra carriage-returns where appropriate.

When writing a follow-up article, most news reader programs allow you to include portions of the original article as quotes. This may be useful if you wish to write separate responses to each point in the original article. However, do not overdo it – it can be very tedious to read articles that consist mostly of quotes from earlier articles. Such articles are usually rather confusing to the reader, especially for anyone who has not followed the thread since its beginning. You should not post a follow-up article that is really only of interest to the person who posted the original article. Instead, you should e-mail your response to that person. It is also important to have your facts straight when posting articles. Much aggravation can be caused by posting inaccurate information, and tends to elicit rude replies from other newsgroup readers.

Since the majority of newsgroup articles still tend to originate from North America, articles are commonly littered with acronyms and other abbreviations that you are expected to understand, such as IMHO (in my humble opinion), FAQ (frequently asked questions), FYI (for your information), BTW (by the way), CU (see you / bye), Objoke (obligatory joke follows), WRT (with respect to) and RTFM (read the *** manual)! For a new user, these may be a little puzzling. If you really must use these, try and stick to the well-known ones.

You may also come across what are called 'smilies' within messages, such as the basic :-) and the depressed :-(face. Look at these by turning the book 90 degrees clockwise. They are used within messages to indicate humour, sadness and other emotions. If you capitalise words LIKE THIS, it means that these words are shouted! Using asterisks like *this* is a way of emphasising particular words.

When finishing an article, people commonly use their newsreader program to create a signature. Although it can be fun to have pictures and witty quotes in your signature, other people will quickly tire of them if you make a lot of postings, so keep them as brief as possible.

Network News is open to many millions of people, is largely unregulated and provides a certain degree of social anonymity to contributors, since you are very unlikely ever to meet most of them. When reading Network News, you will often come across what is called a 'flame', which is an unreasonably aggressive and even abusive response to an earlier message. Some threads seem to consist almost entirely of flame messages, particularly in some of the alt newsgroups. Some people enjoy posting deliberately provocative and controversial articles, in order to attract flame follow-ups, and hence these messages are called 'flame-bait'. Two or more people may get involved in exchanging 'flame' messages, in which case, we have what is called a 'flame war'. Sometimes these flames are clearly not very serious and may even be vaguely humorous, in a black or sarcastic way. However, at other times they can be quite 'close to the bone' and it is possible that people may be seriously offended. Some readers of Network News are amused by flames, whilst most are not. In general, it is not recommended that flames be posted or responded to, since they are neither constructive nor intelligent, and only serve to waste resources on the network.

For more detailed information and discussion about what Network News is, and what it is not, it is worth having a look at the newsgroup news.announce.newusers.

Electronic Mail
One of the greatest benefits of using the Internet is the ease with which you can communicate with other people who are also connected. Messages sent via the Internet from one user to another are called electronic mail, or 'e-mail' for short.

You will come across e-mail when using the Web. For example, you will commonly see e-mail addresses given on Web pages. The address could be that of the Web page author, a company, or simply an address to which you can send e-mail in order to get more information. E-mail addresses also appear in articles submitted to Network News. The address in a newsgroup article usually belongs to the author of that article, so that you may send an e-mail message in response to the article, directly to the author.

E-mail is sent and received using a mail program, sometimes called a 'mailer'. Some Web browsers have a rudimentary mailer facility, but in general it is best to get a dedicated mail program for your Mac or PC. E-mail is received by a 'mail server' computer, and stored until the recipient is ready to read it. E-mail is usually sent using a network communication language, or protocol, called SMTP (Simple Mail Transfer Protocol).

There are a number of shareware and commercial mailer programs available for Macintoshes and PCs. Most of these can be used within a LAN and with the Internet, and offer similar facilities. If you are a LAN user, check with your system administrator to find out what package he or she thinks is most appropriate for your use. If you are going to use a commercial e-mail service of the type provided by a BBS, then the BBS administrators will recommend an appropriate package to use. Popular e-mail programs for PCs and Macintoshes include Microsoft *Mail*, *Pegasus Mail* and Qualcomm *Eudora*.

To send e-mail, the sender types a message in at their computer keyboard, using their mail program. Outgoing messages automatically contain the date and sender's address, which allows the sender to get straight on with writing the message. A

> **Netscape Hint**
>
> You can send e-mail whilst reading Network News, to posters of articles, as described in the previous section. You cannot receive e-mail using *Netscape*, however. For that you will need a dedicated e-mail program. Before sending e-mail with *Netscape*, you must give the browser the IP host name of your SMTP mail server, your name, e-mail address, and organisation. Select Options > Preferences... > Mail. Enter your details into the appropriate fields. If you do not know the IP host name of your SMTP mail server, or your e-mail address, ask your Internet provider. You may also append your name, address and any other details you wish, onto the end of outgoing e-mail and articles to newsgroups. Simply create a simple text file and save it onto disk, using a text editor program such as Apple *SimpleText* or Microsoft *Write*. Signature files should be no more than 4 lines long, if possible. Then in *Netscape*, Select Options > Preferences... > Mail. Depending on your version of *Netscape*, switch on the radio button adjacent to 'File:'. Press the 'Browse' button in order to find and select the text file you created, which is to be used as the signature file.

typical e-mail message may only be a few lines, since it is conventional for e-mail messages to be much less wordy and formal than most ordinary letters. However, there is no need to keep messages short, and it is usually possible to send several pages of text. Most mailers have a maximum limit on the size of an e-mail message, but this is usually large enough for most people.

It is also possible to attach ordinary computer files to your message, which might contain text, spreadsheets, images, sound, video, or other data. This is also a good way of getting around the maximum size limit of an e-mail message, mentioned above. These files are called 'attachments' or 'enclosures'. They are automatically coded by the mailer before being sent, using ASCII characters. Commonly used codes are BinHex and MIME (Multipurpose Internet Mail Extensions). When the attachment is received at the other end, it is decoded by the other mailer

program (presuming it can handle the particular code that has been used). The file can then be saved by the recipient on their hard disc for later use.

Once an e-mail message has been typed into the mail program, and the recipient's e-mail address has been entered, the message is ready to send. It is usually possible to enter more than one address, if desired, so that the message can be sent simultaneously to different recipients. Often, there is an option to keep a copy of every outgoing message for later reference.

Once e-mail has been sent, it can take anything from a few seconds to a few hours to reach its destination, depending on the distance the message must travel, how many computers it is routed through, and how fast those computers process e-mail. Occasionally, a crucial computer link is out of action for a while, in which case an e-mail message may take a day or so whilst it is either re-routed, or temporarily stored.

On arrival the e-mail message will be stored on an Internet host computer which acts as your mail server computer. When you start up your PC or Mac, run your mail program and connect to the mail server, you will be able to access any e-mail that has arrived. E-mail messages may normally either be transferred from the server to your computer, or left on the server. In the first case, you will help to stop the server hard discs filling up with e-mail messages, which is a good thing, but then e-mail transferred to your computer is less secure, if you share your computer with other users. E-mail left on the server is more secure, since it can only be accessed by someone with the right username and password. The recipient of e-mail can choose to either keep or destroy the message, or forward it to another person on the Internet. If they wish to reply to the message, they will normally be able to use the automatic reply facility in their mail program, which looks at the original message to find out where the reply should be sent.

An e-mail address is usually of the form *username@ hostname*. For example, if the full Internet host name of my mail server computer is *glg.ed.ac.uk*, and my user name is *danbishop* then my full e-mail address would be *danbishop@glg.ed.ac.uk*. The part to the left of the @ symbol is often called the mailbox name, so my mailbox name would be danbishop. For some Internet users, their mailbox name is not the same as their user name, so make sure you use the correct

mailbox name. When e-mailing other people, or giving other people your e-mail address, make sure you get the address exactly right, or you are likely to have problems. Do not include extra spaces or punctuation, and take care not to interchange lower case letters for upper case letters. Valid mailbox names can contain letters, numerals, and punctuation such as full-stops and underscores, but not commas, spaces or brackets. If you really must include these forbidden characters in the mailbox name, then enclose the address in double quotes (" ").

Sometimes you will see a percentage sign in the middle of the mailbox name, e.g. *markus%macs@castle.ed.ac.uk*. In this example, any e-mail sent to this address would initially be sent to the host *castle.ed.ac.uk*. The castle computer would then pass it on to *macs*, a server for a Macintosh LAN connected to *castle*. The e-mail message would then be stored on the *macs* server machine until the user *markus* logged-in. So, the percentage sign is just a way of getting the host computer to pass the e-mail message on elsewhere. The e-mail message is said to have 'bounced' off the host machine, which in the above example, is called *castle*.

You will often see e-mail addresses given on Web pages. Sometimes, you will notice they are highlighted, and can be selected like any other hypertext link. Sometimes the links manifest themselves as Web page buttons. When you do this, your browser will start up its mailer facility (providing it has one), and you will be prompted to write a short e-mail message. When you have finished writing your message, the browser will then send the message. The hypertext link provides the e-mail address for the message to be sent to, using a URL format. The format is usually *mailto:username@hostname*. Hence this is sometimes called a 'mailto' facility. Sometimes you will see e-mail addresses given on Web pages which are not highlighted. In this situation you may be able to use your browser to open a new URL, and when prompted, enter *mailto:* followed by the e-mail address. If your browser does not support *mailto:*, then you will have to copy the e-mail address into a dedicated mailer program, and use that program to send the e-mail message.

For most Internet users at universities and other academic institutions, the use of all e-mail is free to the users, which is why e-mail is such a popular way for academics to communicate. You will only be liable for some expense if you are using e-mail

via a commercial Internet vendor. However, using e-mail does not place a great strain on the resources of commercial Internet vendors, compared to the other services that they generally offer, and hence the costs of e-mail are usually minimal. Certainly, e-mail charges should be a lot less than sending ordinary mail by post, or faxes, as well as being much quicker.

E-mail messages are rarely as formal in style and content as letters. It is almost unknown to start a message with the salutation 'Dear Sir' or 'Dear Madam'. Usually 'Dear Fred', 'Fred', 'Hello', or 'Hi' will do, depending on how well you know the person concerned. Instead of signing off with 'Yours Sincerely' or similar, it is more usual to finish more casually, with 'Regards', 'Best Wishes' or similar. Many people create a standard 'signature' using their e-mail program, which is then automatically appended to every message that they send. Signatures should

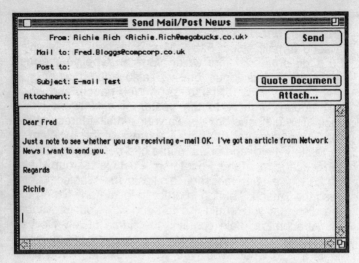

Sending e-mail using the Netscape browser

be short, no more than 4 or 5 lines at the most, and should include useful information such as your full name, organisation, postal address, telephone number, fax number and e-mail address. The latter is often useful should the return-address in the header of your out-going message get scrambled, or cannot be correctly read by the reply facility of your correspondent's e-mail program.

There are really very few rules when it comes to sending e-mail messages. When writing messages, simply observe common-sense courtesy and etiquette. Never write anything which is malicious, or include sensitive information in your messages. E-mail is generally not very secure. In theory your messages may be read by strangers and possibly people you do know, as it is routed from one computer to another, through the Internet.

One important point to remember is: do not pass on e-mail chain letters. At any time, there are a number of these e-mail letters circulating on the Internet, which pretend to offer 'get-rich-quick' schemes, also known as 'pyramid' schemes. Not only are pyramid schemes illegal, they do not work. They also use Internet resources unnecessarily. Furthermore, forwarding

e-mail chain letters to your Internet friends and acquaintances may annoy them, or at the very least they may think less of you for doing so. Beware of scams on the Internet at all times, whether using e-mail, Network News or the Web.

Telnet

Telnet is a very simple way of connecting your PC or Macintosh via a network to a remote computer, which is typically a computer using a Unix operating system. The Telnet method uses TCP/IP and is suitable for the Internet, as well as most LANs. A Telnet client program requires that you specify the Internet address of the remote computer, a username and a password. If you can do this, you can connect to the remote computer, and use that computer as if you were actually sitting at that computer's keyboard.

Telnet client programs provide 'terminal emulation', meaning that they create a window on your Macintosh or PC that looks like an old fashioned terminal screen. There are a variety of terminal types, the most common being the VT100 standard, but they are all typically monochrome and text-only. They cannot display graphics. Therefore, Telnet programs provide only very simple, monochrome, text-only displays, which are quite unlike the Web.

Occasionally, you will see Telnet links embedded in Web pages. The Web page should also give you the appropriate username to use when you connect to a Telnet host, and if necessary, the password also. Telnet links from Web pages use the URL format *telnet://hostname*, for example:

telnet://locis.loc.gov:23/

Note that in this example, the host is accessed via port number 23. When you select a Telnet link from a Web page, your browser will either use an in-built Telnet facility, or start a separate Telnet program. There are a number of freeware and shareware Telnet programs available for PCs and Macintoshes. PC Telnet applications include *EWAN, NCSA Telnet*, Trumpet *Telnet*, *WinQVT, WinTelnet* and *Yawtel*. Macintosh applications include NCSA *Telnet* and *ZTerm*.

The Telnet method of Internet connection is used extensively for connecting to computerised library catalogues, called OPACs (On-line Public Access Catalogues), and also for some interactive services on the Internet which require high-speed access and exchange of information, unhampered by the transfer of images and graphics. The method is also used for accessing older computer archives, which do not yet provide Web access.

It is also possible to connect to some remote computers which will act as rudimentary Web browsers, but which provide no graphic images. This may be useful, if for some reason you cannot use a PC or Macintosh browser, but you do have a Telnet program for your computer. Servers which provide a Web service accessible via Telnet include those listed below:

www.njit.edu	USA
info.cern.ch	Switzerland
info.funet.fi	Finland
vms.huji.ac.il	Israel

If you are asked for a username when connecting to these Web services, use 'www'. Passwords are not required. Once you are connected, you are presented with a welcome page. Typically, the cursor can be moved to the desired link word using the *tab* key on your PC or Macintosh, or the arrow keys, and the link word is selected by pressing *return* or *enter*. If the links are displayed as numbers inside brackets, then enter the relevant

number. Important control keys are usually displayed at the bottom of each page of information. When you select a link, the relevant page is displayed on your screen.

FTP

FTP stands for File Transfer Protocol, and as its name suggests, it is a method of moving computer files across a TCP/IP network, such as the Internet, or most LANs. The files may contain almost any kind of data, including text, programs, images, sound and video. Files may contain data in either one of two main formats: ASCII format or binary format. The protocol requires that you specify the Internet address of the remote computer, a user-name and a password. If you can do this, you can connect to the remote computer, and transfer files across the network.

There are many computers on the Internet that have been especially set up as file archives, which can be accessed by any member of the public, using what is termed 'anonymous' FTP. This term refers to the fact that the username that is used to connect to the archive via FTP is always 'anonymous'. The pass-word required for most anonymous FTP sites is usually your e-mail address, in order that the remote system can identify who is transferring the files. When connected to an anonymous FTP site, which files and directories you can access, and transfer to your computer, i.e. download, will normally be restricted. There may also be some directories on the archive that you can send files to, i.e. upload from your computer.

Hypertext links to Internet computer archives which use FTP are commonly found on Web pages. A typical URL for a FTP server looks like this:

ftp://ftp.austin.apple.com/

This URL identifies a directory on a computer at Apple Computers, which may be accessed via anonymous FTP. When you select a hypertext link such as this one, your browser will automatically connect you to the remote computer, and log you in to the system with the username 'anonymous', and a pass-word which is your e-mail address. It will then present you with a file directory, which will look like a Web page. From this you can select other directories, or by selecting a file, you can download it using FTP.

Sometimes you will see hypertext links on Web pages which point directly to a specific file. For example:

ftp://ftp.med.cornell.edu/pub/jpegview/jpegview33.sit.hqx

In this case, when the link is selected, the browser will automatically connect you to the remote computer with the Internet name *ftp.med.cornell.edu*, log you in as 'anonymous', and send your e-mail address as a password, select the directory */pub/jpegview/* and then download the file *jpegview33.sit.hqx* onto your computer's hard disc (what to do with *.hqx* files is discussed later in this section).

You can also use a variation of the URL format described above, in order to access a private user account on a remote Internet computer, rather than a public anonymous FTP archive. For example:

ftp://bishop@nimrod.ed.ac.uk/

In this fictitious example, the URL points to a user account named *bishop* on the computer with the Internet host name *nimrod.ed.ac.uk*. Unless this account has previously been set up for anonymous access, the user will still have to enter the correct password, before a FTP access may be made.

Another URL form is:

file://ftp.med.cornell.edu/pub/jpegview/jpegview33.sit.hqx

The access method *file* in this URL is synonymous with *ftp* in the previous example. Again, the URL identifies and downloads a file called *jpegview33.sit.hqx* in the directory */pub/jpegview/* on the computer with the IP host name *ftp.med.cornell.edu*. The *file* method is most commonly used to specify a source located on your own computer, rather than a source on another Internet computer. A source on a PC might look something like this:

file:///C:/text/book.txt

This example points to a resource which is a file called *book.txt*, located in a directory called *text*, on a disc drive called C. Note that when using file: a hostname need not be specified. A source

on a Macintosh might look something like this:

file:///Hard%20Disk/text/book

The only difference here is that the name of the disc drive happens to be 'Hard Disk'. Since spaces are not allowed in URLs, the space is represented instead by the code '%20'.

Most browsers provide in-built FTP facilities, so that they can handle hypertext links to FTP sites. However, there are also dedicated FTP programs which can be used on their own to connect to FTP sites. Commonly used FTP applications for PCs include *WsFTP* and *WinFTP*. For Macintosh users, *Fetch* is very popular.

Netscape Hint
The *Netscape* browser has in-built FTP capabilities. Simply select a Web link to the FTP site, or select File > Open Location... and enter the URL. When you connect to an FTP site, anonymous log-in is handled automatically by Netscape. Note that compared with Web pages, an FTP directory display has minimal formatting. In addition, *Netscape* usually shows the type, size, date and a short description of each file in a directory. Downloading of files via FTP is also handled automatically by *Netscape*. What happens to downloaded files depends on how you have set your Preferences. For any given file type you may be prompted to decide what to do with it. You may choose to save the file to disc, you may use *Netscape* to view it, or you may launch a helper application to handle the file. See the section on helper applications in Chapter 2.

If you are using a browser to handle FTP transfer, the browser will automatically choose whether to download a file in ASCII or binary format. If you are using a dedicated FTP program you may have to choose which form of transfer is most appropriate to the kind of file you are transferring. In general, most files available for transfer via FTP are binary format files. The notable exceptions include: all text files, which commonly have the file extension *.txt*, or file names like *readme* and *index*;

FTP Directory: ftp://wuarchive.wustl.edu/

[FILE] README .... [Nov 6 13:31]   2k

[FILE] README.NFS .... [Nov 6 13:41]   1k

[LINK] SimTel .... [Nov 10 11:06]

[DIR] bin .... [Oct 21 13:28]

[DIR] decus .... [Oct 22 20:07]

[DIR] doc .... [Nov 10 11:10]

[DIR] edu .... [Oct 14 12:41]

[DIR] etc .... [Dec 1 12:52]

[DIR] graphics .... [Oct 22 19:12]

[DIR] info .... [Dec 29 04:49]

[DIR] languages .... [Oct 20 19:34]

[DIR] mirrors .... [Oct 21 13:27]

[DIR] multimedia .... [Oct 18 23:05]

[DIR] packages .... [Nov 27 13:50]

[DIR] pub .... [Dec 27 20:57]

Viewing a directory at an anonymous FTP site, using Netscape

and *BinHex* files, which have the file extension *.hqx* (see later this section for more on BinHex).

Some files may be used immediately after they have been downloaded across the Internet. For example, image, sound and video files can usually be opened using the appropriate application for the format, as described in Chapter 2. Less commonly, you may be able to download PC and Macintosh program files and run them immediately. Executable PC files may be recognised by the file name extension *.exe*. However, most program files on Internet archives are in a coded and compressed state, which means that before you can use such a file, you must decode and decompress it first. Compressed files take up less space in the Internet archive. Also, when such compressed files

are transferred by FTP, the transfer between computers takes less time, and there is much less strain on Internet resources. Commonly several files, and/or directories, are amalgamated and compressed into one file.

Some FTP applications (e.g. *Fetch*) are capable of carrying out some decoding for you, as they download the file. Others do not, and browsers in particular do not normally have in-built decoding and decompression facilities. They rely on external, dedicated decoding and decompression programs being available.

In principle, PC files and Macintosh files can generally be compressed and archived using the same compression formats. For example, *PKZip* compressed archives may be created for both PC and Macintosh files. Thus, in theory, a file extension *.zip* indicates only that it is a PKZip compressed archive, not whether it is a Macintosh or a PC file. This is true of most of the major compression formats. However, in practice, Macintosh files are usually compressed in different formats from PC files, can be distinguished by their file extensions, and are decompressed using different utility programs. In most cases, files with the extension *.zip* are PC files.

For a *.zip* file, you will need a PC decompression program such as *PKUnzip* or *WinZip*. You may also come across other file extensions which indicate that the file is probably a PC file. Other file extensions which indicate that you need to decompress them before you can use them include *.arc* (needs *Arc* or *PKPak*), *.arj* (needs *Arj*), *.lzh* (needs *LHArc*), *.pak* (needs *Pak*), *.zoo* (needs *Zoo*). Sometimes you will come across PC files encoded using the BinHex format, although it is more commonly used for Macintosh files. BinHex files often have the file extension *.hqx*. A good program that may be used to decode BinHex on a PC is the shareware *Windows* program *WinCode*. This utility will also decode files in the UUencode format, which usually have the file name extension *.uue*.

Some files which you may download may be self-extracting archives, which means that you do not need a decompression program. You can simply execute the self-extracting archive (by typing its name at the DOS prompt, or by clicking on its name in the *Windows* File Manager). Once executed, the file will decompress itself, often into several separate files. Like any executable PC file, PC self-extracting archives usually have the file name

extension .*exe*.

Macintosh files can usually be recognised by distinctive file extensions, most commonly .*hqx*, .*cpt*, .*sit*, .*bin* and .*gz*. The .*gz* extension means that the computer at the FTP site will automatically do the first stage of decompression when the file is transferred. Many Macintosh files on FTP archives are coded using BinHex, and therefore have the file extension .*hqx*. A program called BinHex will decode a BinHex file, although it will not do any further decompression that may be necessary. More useful programs are the freeware application *StuffIt Expander*, and the shareware application *Compact Pro*. These two utilities will not only decode BinHex, but will also decode and decompress .*cpt* files (*Compact Pro* format). *StuffIt Expander* will also handle .*bin* files (MacBinary format) and .*sit* files (*StuffIt* format). A shareware application from the makers of *StuffIt Expander*, called *DropStuff with Expander Enhancer*, enables you to decode UUencoded files, which have the file name extension .*uue*. It will also decode a variety of other formats less commonly used for Macintosh files. Sometimes you will come across the Macintosh file extension .*sea*, which stands for 'self extracting archive'. When you execute this file, it will decompress itself automatically.

The .*lha* file extension is commonly used for compacted Amiga computer files. Unix files commonly have file extensions .*Z*, .*tar* or .*TAR*, and thus if you are a PC or Macintosh user, these files are unlikely to be of interest.

Remember that files transferred by FTP may carry computer viruses, as discussed at the end of this chapter. Always check a new file that you have downloaded with a virus protection utility program to make sure that it is not infected. If it is infected, either fix it with the virus protection program, or delete the file.

Gopher

Gopher is a method of retrieving information across a network. It was originally designed to provide a campus-wide information system at the University of Minnesota Microcomputer, Workstation, Networks Center in 1991. Since then it has been adapted for use on the Internet.

Gopher servers allow you to make choices from menus, not dissimilar to some Web pages. Gopher provides good keyword search mechanisms, and also provides facilities for downloading

files. However, unlike the Web, Gopher is not graphically orient-
ed, but is instead a text based system. All interaction with a
Gopher system is menu based, so there is little of the flexibility
found in the Web.

However, there are still plenty of Gopher servers connected to
the Internet, and it is common to come across Web pages with
hypertext links to Gopher servers. An example of a URL for a
Gopher resource would be:

gopher://veronica.scs.unr.edu/11/veronica

In this example, the URL points to a popular Gopher program
called veronica (Very Easy Rodent-Orientated Net-wide Index to
Computerised Archives), which is a utility developed for searching Gopher archives. This program's name is usually spelled
with a lower-case 'v'.

Most browsers have a built-in facility for handling Gopher
resources. They will automatically connect you to a Gopher
server and log you in with the correct username, if any is
required. Common usernames are 'gopher' and 'info'. You can
then move from Gopher menu to Gopher menu, do keyword
searches and download files.

Netscape Hint
The *Netscape* browser has in-built capability to connect to
Gopher sites. Simply select a Web link to the site, or select
File > Open Location... and enter the URL. Like FTP sites,
but unlike Web sites, Gopher sites do not produce richly formatted pages. You can follow Gopher links to image, sound
and video sources, and download files, in the same way
that you can with FTP. Gopher sites will also commonly
offer you search facilities, such as *veronica*, and *Netscape*
will provide you with dialogue boxes where you can enter
keywords to search for.

There are also dedicated Gopher client applications available
for Macintoshes and PCs. Gopher client applications for PCs
include *WinGopher*, *WsGopher* and *Hgopher*. Macintosh

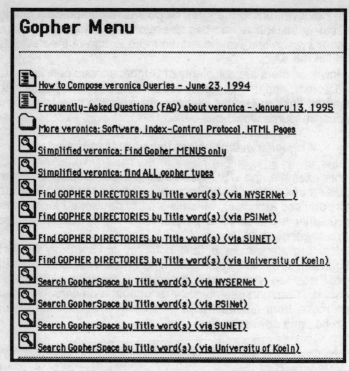

Gopher Menu

📄 How to Compose veronica Queries - June 23, 1994

📄 Frequently-Asked Questions (FAQ) about veronica - January 13, 1995

📁 More veronica: Software, Index-Control Protocol, HTML Pages

🔍 Simplified veronica: Find Gopher MENUS only

🔍 Simplified veronica: find ALL gopher types

🔍 Find GOPHER DIRECTORIES by Title word(s) (via NYSERNet)

🔍 Find GOPHER DIRECTORIES by Title word(s) (via PSINet)

🔍 Find GOPHER DIRECTORIES by Title word(s) (via SUNET)

🔍 Find GOPHER DIRECTORIES by Title word(s) (via University of Koeln)

🔍 Search GopherSpace by Title word(s) (via NYSERNet)

🔍 Search GopherSpace by Title word(s) (via PSINet)

🔍 Search GopherSpace by Title word(s) (via SUNET)

🔍 Search GopherSpace by Title word(s) (via University of Koeln)

A Gopher menu accessed using Netscape

Gopher applications include *MacGopher*, *Turbo Gopher*, *GopherApp* and *PNL Info Browser*.

WAIS
Another method of retrieving information from some Internet computers is called WAIS (Wide Area Information Servers). It was developed before the Web, by Apple, KPMG Peat Marwick, Dow Jones and Thinking Machines. The original developers have now formed their own company, WAIS Inc. WAIS is quite an efficient system for extracting information from very large databases, since not only does it search document titles, but also document contents. However, like Gopher, WAIS is a text-based system, and is somewhat limited in scope compared to the Web.

Although WAIS servers are much less common than Gopher servers, you will occasionally see hypertext links on Web pages to WAIS resources. An example of a URL for a WAIS resource is:

wais://ds.internic:210/conf.announce

Note that in this example a port number is specified for the WAIS server computer, which happens to be 210. Some Web browsers handle WAIS connections automatically. They will connect you to the WAIS server, and log you on using an appropriate username, if needed, such as 'wais' or 'swais'. You can then conduct searches using keywords, and view matching documents which are retrieved from the WAIS archives. There are also dedicated WAIS client programs available for PCs and Macintoshes, notably *WinWAIS* and *MacWAIS*.

Netscape Hint
WAIS connections are not handled by *Netscape*.

Virus Warning
Computer viruses are programs, usually quite small, that are so called because they behave in a similar way to the viruses caught by humans and other animals. They are capable of self-replication and are good at disguising themselves. Worst of all, they can be very destructive. Viruses are written by anarchic programmers around the world, who seem to get some sense of satisfaction from spreading misery amongst the rest of us. Although virus creation borders on being a criminal activity, it is practically impossible to locate the perpetrators. Furthermore, since viruses replicate themselves, they can, in theory, survive almost indefinitely in a large population of computers. Some common viruses have been around for many years.

Most computer viruses spread via the interchange of floppy discs between computers, although they can be transmitted via networks such as the Internet. Some viruses can only exist on floppy discs, whilst others can copy themselves onto your hard discs. Viruses commonly disguise themselves by 'hiding' in

certain sectors of a floppy disc, or by attaching themselves to another program file, which in itself may be harmless. Thus, if a program file is found to be larger than it should be, this may indicate that a virus has attached itself.

One advantage of using the Web to explore the Internet is that viruses cannot be caught by viewing a Web page, so visit as many Web pages as you wish without fear. This is because Web pages are not executable files, but merely comprise a series of codes used to produce a display on your computer screen. Similarly, it is not possible to infect your computer with a virus by reading an e-mail message. Again, in simple terms, an e-mail message is only a collection of text characters which are displayed on your screen. E-mail messages are not executable files. At the time of writing there was an e-mail message in circulation on the Internet purporting that there was another message around that could infect your computer, called "Good Times", but the message is now widely acknowledged as a hoax.

However, if you choose to download any kind of program or other executable file onto your computer from a Web page, or from any Internet source, you run the risk of downloading a virus along with the file. The virus may become active when you execute the file. Luckily, viruses are not too common on reputable Internet sites, but they are out there, so be cautious. As described below, check all downloaded programs using a virus protection program, before using them. Also, only use reputable Internet sources.

Viruses manifest themselves in a variety of ways too numerous to describe, since the number of viruses in circulation increases by several hundred every month, and there are now more than 6000 known viruses. Fortunately, few of them are very common. They sometimes remain dormant until some particular operation is carried out on your computer, or they may wait for a certain date to arrive before activating (they can do this by querying the on-board computer clock). When they are activated they may do something relatively harmless, such as print a rude message on the screen. More commonly they will scramble other files on a disc, or cause problems when saving files.

There are now a whole host of programs available that can detect and destroy viruses. The most commonly used ones are freeware, and available from anonymous FTP archives on the Internet. Virus protection programs may also be bought. If your

computer is part of a network, your network administrator will almost definitely be able to provide you with a virus protection program. Well-known Macintosh virus protection programs include *Disinfectant* and *Sam Intercept*. Comparable programs for PC users include *F-PROT*, *AntiVirus Toolkit*, *Thunderbyte Anti-Virus* and *Norton Anti-Virus*.

Once installed, you can typically run a virus protection program at any time, and instruct it to scan your hard disc, floppy discs, and computer memory for viruses. Most virus protection programs can also be set up so that they check your hard discs and memory every time your computer starts up. They may check any floppy discs that are inserted, and will regularly check memory. They are capable of recognising a very wide variety of viruses, and at your command will generally be able to destroy them and repair your discs and files. Some programs will also spot new viruses and pieces of suspicious code that just might be a new virus. In this case, they will warn you, even though they may be unable to do anything about it.

The importance of having a virus protection program installed on your computer cannot be over-stressed. More than that, you should make sure that it is properly installed and used regularly. Be particularly sure to keep all your floppy discs free of viruses, and check any new ones that you get. Even brand new floppy discs have been known to contain viruses, although this is rare, and if you use only reputable brands you should be safe. Check all programs and other executable files downloaded from the Internet. Viruses are much more common on PCs than Macintoshes, but users of both should take care. Not only are you protecting yourself and your own system, but you are also stopping the spread of viruses.

Chapter 4

THE KEY WEB PAGES

Software Archives

In this section we describe some of the most popular Internet software archives of Macintosh and PC software. All of these sites may be reached via the Web, and many of them can also be reached via anonymous FTP. URLs for Web and anonymous FTP access are given. Many of these sites provide Web software, including browsers and helper applications, as well as many other types of programs. Many also provide images, sounds, and video, and other kinds of data files.

Whilst much of the software available on these sites is freeware, much of it is not. When you download software, check to see if you must register the package and if you must send payment to the producers of the software. Also, whilst it is the authors' opinion that all the sites listed here are very reputable, we cannot provide a guarantee that all downloaded files will be free of viruses. It is always sensible to check downloaded files using a good virus protection program (see Chapter 3).

CICA

http://www.cica.indiana.edu/index.html
ftp://cica.cica.indiana.edu/pub
There is a major software archive at the Center for Innovative Computer Applications (CICA), Indiana. Programs are available for PCs and Macintoshes, and there are a variety of other resources also available at this site.

CSUSM Windows World

http://coyote.csusm.edu/cwis/winworld/winworld.html
ftp://ftp.csusm.edu/pub/winworld/
A searchable archive of Windows software. Files are also listed by category.

SunSITE Northern Europe

http://src.doc.ic.ac.uk/
ftp://src.doc.ic.ac.uk/
A major software archive located at Imperial College in London.

This is a fast and reliable source, particularly recommended for those in the UK. Most freeware and shareware, PC and Macintosh programs may be found on this archive. There are also collections of software from other Internet archives (mirrors).

The Well Connected Mac
http://www.macfaq.com/
A useful Macintosh software archive with rudimentary file search facilities. There is a link to a 'Mac site of the moment', and there are also competitions to be entered. There is a searchable directory of vendors doing business in the Macintosh market, although they are mostly in the USA. There are FAQs and links for all the Macintosh newsgroups. Macintosh software and hardware reviews are also available.

Ultralab
http://www.ultralab.anglia.ac.uk/
ftp://ftp.ultralab.anglia.ac.uk/
A source of information on the use of computers and the Internet in schools. Also a source of commercial and freeware educational software, much of it for Macintosh computers.

Utexas Mac Archive
http://wwwhost.ots.utexas.edu/mac/main.html
ftp://ftp.utexas.edu/pub/mac
An impressive archive of Macintosh software held at the University of Texas, which contains almost every imaginable freeware and shareware program.

Virtual Software Library
http://vsl.cnet.com/
Not actually a software archive in its own right, but rather a very powerful tool for finding software on a number of popular Internet archives, including cica, sim-win3, sim-nt, sim-msdos, garbo-pc, ms-softlib, netwire, pcga, cd-games, hobbes-os2, umi-mac, info-mac, aminet, umi-atari, linux, tsx11, sim-ux, garbo-ux, alt.src, c.s.unix, c.s.misc and c.s.x. It is equally good at finding PC and Macintosh software. In addition, when it finds software, it offers you a choice of sites from which you may download the software. Thus you can choose a site near to home, cutting download time and reducing strain on the Internet.

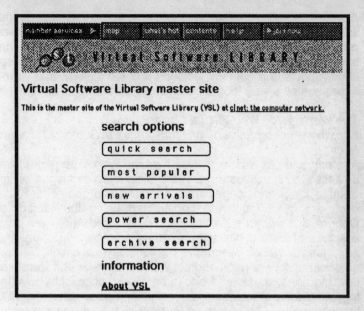

Virtual Software Library

Useful Homepages

There are a number of Web sites which provide useful jumping-off points for exploring the Web, and we give some of them here. One of the easiest ways of finding topics that interest you on the Web is by using a hierarchical subject catalogue, which you can search from the top-down, or search using a keyword search facility. The homepages presented here nearly all provide such catalogues, and are completely free for anyone to use. You might like to set your Web browser preferences so that it downloads your favourite homepage on start-up.

The Whole Internet Catalog
http://nearnet.gnn.com/wic/index.html
An excellent guide to more than 1200 of the best Web sites world wide from O'Reilly, updated from the popular American book "The Whole Internet Catalog User's Guide Catalog". Web pages

are categorised under subject headings, which include: arts and entertainment, business and finance, computers, daily news, education, government and politics, health and medicine, humanities and social sciences, internet, life and culture, recreation, sports and hobbies, science and technology, and travel. There is also a very long alphabetically sorted list of topics.

The World Wide Web Virtual Library
http://www.w3.org/hypertext/DataSources/bySubject/Overview.html
Another guide to what is available on the Web. Web pages may be accessed in various ways. There is a subject catalogue, which is quite long, and ranges from agriculture to zoos.There is a second subject catalogue constructed using the Library of Congress standards, which includes: agriculture, auxiliary sciences of history, bibliography/library science, education, fine arts, general works, geography/anthropology/recreation, history-america, history-general and old world, language and literature, law, medicine, music and books on music, philosophy/psychology/religion, political science, science, social sciences, and technology. You can search an index of all the topics by entering a keyword to look for. There is also a guide to the Internet, with Internet services listed by type of service.

Tradewave Galaxy
http://www.einet.net/galaxy.html
This site provides a very complete guide to what is available on the Web. Web sites are listed in a hierarchical fashion. The main subject headings include: business and commerce, community, engineering and technology, government, humanities, law, leisure and recreation, medicine, reference and interdisciplinary information, science, and social sciences. A search facility enables topics of interest to be quickly identified. This is also the home site for the MacWeb and winWeb browsers.

World Wide Web Consortium
http://www.w3.org/
This is the homepage of the organisation which invented the Web, and is currently steering its development. There are links here to information about what the Web is, its history and how it works. In particular there is information about the developers,

and what the latest innovations are. This is the best site for news on the latest versions of HTML, HTTP and other Web standards. There is also information about the latest international Web conferences.

UKdirectory
http://www.ukdirectory.com/
A guide to everything that's British on the Web. Top level subject headings include business/finance, community services, computers, education, employment, entertainment, politics, personal home pages, news, shopping, sports, telecommunications, and travel. In total there are more than 2,500 listings in this Web guide. There is also an alphabetically sorted list of UK Web sites.

UK Index
http://www.ukindex.co.uk/index.html
A comprehensive guide to the best Web sites in the UK. The list is constantly updated, with many new sites appearing all the time. The list is organised by subjects, but may also be searched using keywords. You can also look at the most recent additions to the database.

UK Index

Yahoo

http://www.yahoo.com/

Yahoo is an acronym for Yet Another Hierarchically Odoriferous Oracle, and is also one of the oldest and most popular home-pages on the Web, with links to virtually any subject imaginable, and some that aren't! The service was originally operated by Stanford University, but has recently gone commercial, like so many other Web sites. Possibly the quickest way to find something is to enter a keyword in the search field on the homepage. Otherwise you can start with the top-level subject catalogue and work your way down the many branches. The top-level subjects are: arts, business and economy, computers and internet, education, entertainment, government, health, news, recreation, reference, regional, science, social science, society and culture. If you cannot decide where you want to go, you can instruct the Yahoo server to send you a random link chosen from its data-base. You can also submit your own favourite URLs for inclusion in the database. Also available at Yahoo is a news service, pro-vided by the international news service Reuters, covering both US and international news, and available by selecting the 'Headlines' link from the Yahoo homepage.

Search Engines

Searching for a topic using subject catalogues is limited because they are only linked to the URLs the administrators have chosen to include, and provide no access to those which they have chosen to leave out, or do not know about. Although the cata-logues given in the previous section are usually updated on a daily basis, they will not always include the newest Web sites. As an alternative to using a subject catalogue to find items of interest on the Web, it is possible to search the Web more direct-ly, using a program known as a search engine. These programs continuously and automatically search the Web for new links to add to their databases. There are several major search engine programs which may be accessed via the Web. In this section, we list several Web pages which provide access to search engines. Simply enter one or more keywords into the form on the search engine Web page, submit your request, and you will receive a new Web page which gives a list of links to Web pages that match your request. Each link found is called a 'hit'. You may

also be able to choose the maximum number of 'hits' returned, and change other parameters which control how the search is conducted.

Aliweb
http://web.nexor.co.uk/aliweb/doc/aliweb.html
This Web site enables you to search the Aliweb database at Nexor, in the UK. Nexor is a technology company that specialises in providing electronic communication software products and services. Use of the Aliweb database is free, however. There are a variety of options you may choose when conducting a keyword search. For example, you can restrict your search to the UK domain, so that only Web sites in the UK are listed. There are mirrors of the Aliweb database in other countries, which may be reached via the URL given above.

Finding People on the Internet
http://www.nova.edu/Inter-Links/phone.html
Finding information about individual Internet users via the Internet is fraught with problems, since there is no central register of all users that may be queried. This Web page is a brave attempt to tackle these problems. It provides several ways of finding an individual through the Internet (assuming that the individual concerned actually uses the Internet). You can:

(1) search for an e-mail address;
(2) use the 'finger' program to identify a user from their e-mail address (many Internet hosts do not support 'finger', so this can be a problem);
(3) search various organisations' phone directories (only a few of which are UK organisations);
(4) search an experimental X.500 directory database;
(5) use the 'whois' program to look up information on an institution using its domain name.

The system works best when finding Internet users in the USA, but even then, the system will commonly not find the information that you want. However, try all the tools available, and with a bit of patience and luck you may be successful.

LookUP!
http://www.lookup.com/
LookUP! is a directory service which enables you to search for e-mail addresses simply by entering the name, and optionally, the location of an individual or organisation. The LookUP! database includes hundreds of thousands of entries and is continuously updated. You can become a member of the service for free. Members get further benefits, namely advanced searching facilities, personal home pages, e-mail programs integrated with LookUP!, and the ability to add names to the database.

Lycos
http://lycos.cs.cmu.edu/
Lycos, at Carnegie Mellon University, has long been a popular stepping stone for exploration of the Web. This site is now commercial and very slick. There is a powerful search facility for finding topics of interest. Lycos has indexed over 7.98 million pages throughout the world, estimated to represent 91% of the entire contents of the Web. To use Lycos, simply enter your keywords into the form on the Lycos homepage. In addition, there are more sophisticated search methods available. Full instructions on how to use these methods are given at this Web site. The 250 Web pages most commonly found by the Lycos search engine are listed under subject headings: business, education, entertainment, reference, government, news, sports, travel, weather, and web resources.

W3 Search Engines
http://cuiwww.unige.ch/meta-index.html
This Web page is not a search engine in itself, but provides links to a number of other search engines, which are listed by categories: information servers, software, people, publications, news/faqs, documentation, and 'other interesting things' (e.g. jargon, acronyms). Simply enter your keyword in the field adjacent to the most appropriate search engine and press the 'submit' button. Be aware that some of the search engines given do not always work, and sometimes when URLs for search engines change, they do not always get updated on this Web page.

WebCrawler
http://webcrawler.com/

Arguably the most reliable, fast and effective search engine available on the Web. The fact that it daily gets more than 1.5 million queries from around the world attests to its popularity. Simply go to this page, enter your keywords, and press the 'search' button. There are other options available too, with which to control your search. It is rare for this search engine not to return something useful. Also, it seems to be equally good at finding Web sites outside the USA as it is finding USA-based sites. Other interesting items at this site include: links to the top 25 most frequently linked URLs on the Web; random Web links for the adventurous; and regularly updated statistics recording the growth and usage of the Web.

World Wide Web Worm
http://www.cs.colorado.edu/home/mcbryan/WWWW.html

Another very powerful and popular search engine, in the same league as WebCrawler. In 1994 Web users voted the WWW Worm the best navigational aid on the Web. The WWW Worm homepage lets you quickly enter keywords and does a fast search based on your entry. There are also a number of search options which may be chosen.

Chapter 5

COMMERCE

Computer Companies

Not surprisingly, producers of computer software and hardware have been quick to establish Web sites on the Internet. These sites typically provide advertising for current and forthcoming products, product specifications, ordering information, software updates, customer support, and information about the companies. In this section we list some of the larger computer companies on the Internet. In addition, homepages of Web software suppliers and developers are given in Appendix 2, and those of Internet vendors in Appendix 3.

Apple
http://www.apple.com

A slick Web site providing all the information you could want about Apple computers. Look here for the latest news on new Macintoshes, Power Macintoshes, PowerBooks and other hardware, such as Newton, Apple's personal digital assistant. There are also product specifications for Apple network systems and printers. Freeware software and software patches from Apple are available for downloading, plus ordering information for other software products, such as Apple's multimedia system QuickTime. There is also information about forthcoming products, such as the much vaunted new Macintosh operating system, codenamed Copland, and virtual reality products such as QuickTime VR. From this Web site you can also access and find out more about eWorld, Apple's BBS, which provides Apple technical support, as well as electronic mail, 'chat rooms', and other information.

Compaq
http://www.compaq.com/

All you need to know about the PC manufacturing giant, Compaq, including their latest PC models, Microsoft Windows 95, and their initiatives in education and business.

DEC

http://www.digital.com

A very image intensive Web site, this is the homepage for the Digital Equipment Corporation, best known for their Alpha workstations, which run both Unix and VMS. They also produce high-performance PC workstations, which run Microsoft *Windows*. Everything you need to know about the company and its products is here.

Dell

http://www.dell.com

The Dell Computer Corporation Web site provides information about their latest desktop and laptop PCs. There is also information about customer support and many other aspects of the company.

Hewlett-Packard

http://www.hp.com

Here you can find out everything about American computer giant, Hewlett-Packard, famous for producing printers, plotters, scanners, high-performance workstations, and scientific equipment. There is plenty on this site about HP's latest hardware and software products.

IBM

http://www.ibm.com

This is the corporate homepage of IBM, which provides links to all IBM's computing and software products and services, world wide. A novel feature is that you can select your country of preference, (e.g. UK) from a pull-down menu, in order to get local IBM information. The IBM UK pages are extensive, covering everything from the latest IBM British product releases, to the location of local IBM offices (with maps). There is information on IBM's initiatives in education in British schools. You can download various bits of software too, such as drivers and patches for *OS/2 Warp*. On many of the IBM Web pages you are given the opportunity to send feedback or questions to IBM, either via forms or via e-mail. Also, from the IBM homepage you can follow links to the IBM Network, which is IBM's own BBS.

Intel
http://www.intel.com
This site contains a wealth of information on Intel, a major computer hardware producer, best known for its various processors, such as Pentium processors, which lie at the heart of many PCs. At this site there is also P6 and other processor information. Intel also make video conferencing, networking and modem products. This Web site offers pages about the company, its finances and job opportunities with Intel.

Microsoft
http://www.microsoft.com
This is the starting point if you want to know anything about Microsoft and its products. There are links here to the latest on *Windows 95*, as well as older versions of *Windows*, including software, such as device drivers and software patches. There is full information on Microsoft's many other software products, such as *Word, Access, Excel, Office*, and *PowerPoint*, plus their many games and leisure programs. There are tables of recommended retail prices, which are worth checking before you go shopping for your next bit of Microsoft software. Recent additions to the Microsoft Web site include information on Microsoft *Internet Explorer*, the official *Windows 95* browser. The browser, which is freeware, may be downloaded from this site. Also, from this site you can follow links to The Microsoft Network, which is Microsoft's own BBS.

Novell
http://www.novell.com
This Web site contains information about Novell, a company best known for its computer network operating systems, and network software. If you use or manage a LAN, you are bound to find much of interest on these pages. They have recently diversified, and now produce a range of software for business and home use, including wordprocessing (*WordPerfect*), spreadsheet (*Quattro Pro*), presentation, and desktop publishing software. They also produce their own flavour of DOS for PCs. Information about the company, software ordering, and other Novell products may also be found at this site.

Seiko-Epson
http://www.epson.co.jp/epson/weleng.htm
Information here about the Seiko-Epson corporation, best known for its timepieces and printer products, including contact details for subsidiaries world wide.

Banks and other Financial Services
Now that a variety of methods have been developed for making secure financial transactions via the Internet, more established financial institutions, including the 'high-street' banks, are offering Web services, as well as the many recently established companies which have appeared since the development of the Web. Furthermore, the Web presents an ideal way of rapidly disseminating information about current international exchange rates, money and stock market data.

BankNet
http://mkn.co.uk/bank
BankNet Electronic Banking Service is a UK-based Internet banking service, a joint venture between MarketNet and Secure Trust Bank plc. A BankNet account offers the normal facilities of a current account, i.e. no transaction charges even if overdrawn, interest on credit balances, cheque book, guarantee card, and cash card. In addition, you can open an account via the Web, check your account details at any time via the Web, and you can write 'electronic' cheques (digitally signed cheques using cryptographic techniques). They also offer business accounts. At present, the software for writing 'electronic' cheques is only available for *Windows*.

Bank of Scotland
http://www.bankofscotland.co.uk/
This Web site provides a history of the bank (now 300 years old), together with a large amount of information about its conventional services, such as personal and business accounts, young saver accounts, student and graduate accounts, mortgages, and insurance. The Bank of Scotland also offers electronic banking, via a service called HOBS (Home Office Banking Service). You can connect to the bank's computers using either a PC and a modem, or using a 'screenphone' (a telephone with a built-in

video screen). To access HOBS using a PC and modem you will need a communications software package that supports video-text emulation. HOBS allows you to view your accounts, settle bills electronically without writing cheques, transfer funds between accounts, check standing orders and direct debits, request a pay-in book or statement, and send messages to your branch.

Barclays Bank
http://www.barclays.co.uk/
Full details about Barclays Bank personal and business services are available from this site, including information about the various types of bank accounts available, loans, mortgages, telephone banking, Barclays' stockbrokers, travel insurance, and BarclayCard. There is also a link to a virtual shopping mall, BarclaySquare (see next section). Barclays Bank is also developing an electronic banking service for customers who have a PC and a modem. Soon it will be possible for users of the system to pay bills, analyse interim statements, request account balances, set up and/or change standing orders, and transfer funds between accounts, all from their own PC.

Bradford & Bingley Building Society
http://www.bradford-bingley.co.uk/bbbs/
This Web site provides full details of Bradford & Bingley's conventional services, including mortgages, insurance, pensions, savings and other accounts, and investment oppor-tunities. There is information about the company, and also a useful branch locator facility.

Cheltenham & Gloucester Building Society
http://www.cheltglos.co.uk/
Information here on all of this building society's services. Full details of mortgages are given, and there is a useful guide to buying and selling homes. Location details of all branches are given too.

CyberCash
http://www.cybercash.com

An Internet service which offers clients the ability to make payments via the Internet. CyberCash offers secure credit card payments via the Web, using RSA encryption. Once the desired merchandise has been selected from the Web page, the consumer simply clicks on the CyberCash icon when they are ready to pay. The user selects their preferred credit card from a menu and then clicks on the 'Pay' button. The company hopes to offer electronic cash payments soon and is collaborating with a variety of mainstream financial institutions. CyberCash also maintain a Web page, which lists major banks on the Web, on a country by country basis.

DigiCash
http://www.digicash.com

DigiCash call their form of payment 'ecash', short for 'electronic cash'. DigiCash is currently acting as an Internet bank, although mainstream banks can join the scheme. A user of this system must firstly open an account with Digicash, and make a normal monetary payment to the account so that it is in credit. Withdrawals of ecash from a DigiCash account are made using a password known only to the owner of the account. The ecash is 'downloaded' to the DigiCash client's computer. Then, whenever the DigiCash client wants to make a payment via the Internet, he or she simply sends an electronic code to the payee, which specifies the amount and validity of the ecash. DigiCash use a notional 'coin'-based system, where coins have pre-determined values, each 'signed' by the bank. The buyer combines coins of different values into the amount they want to pay, just like real coins. Ecash payments can be validated, but on their own, cannot be used by anyone to trace the identity of the buyer, just like real cash. Ecash offers one-sided anonymity, since when clearing a transaction only the payee is identified by the bank. The only 'real' monetary transactions occur between the buyer and the bank, and the seller and the bank. If ecash is lost, because it is accidentally deleted from a computer, this is reported to the bank together with the serial numbers of the lost coins. These serial numbers allow the bank to check if the coins are really lost, before refunding the money. The software needed to

use ecash is freely available from DigiCash, for both PCs and Macintoshes.

Foreign Exchange Rates
http://www.dna.lth.se/cgi-bin/kurt/rates
An easy-to-use service which allows you to find the current exchange rate between any two major currencies. Simply select the two desired currencies from the lists given, and you will be given the current exchange rate. Rates are normally updated daily.

Lloyds Bank
http://www.lloydsbank.co.uk/
At present, the only Web service available from Lloyds Bank is Lloyds Bank Campus, which provides a host of information about Lloyds Bank's student and graduate services. Many future developments are promised at this Web site.

MasterCard International
http://www.Mastercard.com
Information about the MasterCard company, various kinds of credit cards available from MasterCard, and MasterCard initiatives in developing smartcards, and protocols for secure financial transactions on the Internet is available at this site. There are also links to Internet shopping malls where you can make purchases over the Internet using MasterCard. An interesting feature is the teller machine locator. Simply enter the city and street name, and it will list the local teller machines which accept MasterCard. Also, there is a simple currency converter page, for which the rates are updated weekly.

Nationwide Building Society
http://www.worldserver.pipex.com/nationwide/homepage/home-page.htm
Nationwide offers a comprehensive range of financial products, including mortgages, loans, savings, banking, and financial reviews. All the information is here. They also offer free spreadsheets for downloading, which can be used for pension calculations, budgetting, etc.

QuoteCom
http://www.quote.com
QuoteCom is a service dedicated to providing financial market data to Internet users. This includes current quotes on stocks, options, commodity futures, mutual funds, and bonds. It also includes business news, market analysis and commentary, fundamental (balance sheet) data, and company profiles. QuoteCom is free for limited use, but you must register in order to gain full use of it.

The Royal Bank of Scotland
http://www.royalbankscot.co.uk/home.htm
Full information on the Royal Bank of Scotland's conventional services for personal and business customers, including various types of accounts, mortgages, investments, financial planning, offshore banking and currency exchange rates.

Visa
http://www.visa.com
These Web pages provide information about the company, and detail the various kinds of credit cards available from Visa. There is news on the development of secure protocols for financial transactions on the Internet, and the full specifications for the STT standard are located here. Also, there are some interesting items about future methods of making payments with smartcards. There is a teller machine locator, which will help you find teller machines that accept Visa world wide. There is also information about Visa's activities internationally, and Visa sponsored events and projects.

Commercial Guides and Virtual Shopping Malls
There are now a large number of Web sites that offer guides to commercial services available via the Web. Most such sites are based in the USA, and provide listings of mainly North American businesses. However, there are now a few commercial guides on the Web which are aimed specifically at the UK market, some of which are listed in this section. Likewise, there are a number of major US-based virtual shopping malls, but some virtual shopping malls are now appearing in the UK too. The Web pages listed below provide links to all the leading shops, services, and

other kinds of businesses in the UK, which are too numerous to mention individually.

Apollo Advertising
http://apollo.co.uk/home.html
Apollo have an advertising service on the Web, used by a variety of commercial services in the UK, and world wide. The system integrates both classified and business advertising. Most advertisements have links to related Web pages. You can search the database of advertisers in a variety of ways. Every search gives results starting with the most recent advertisements at the top.

BarclaySquare
http://www.itl.net/barclaysquare/
A British virtual shopping mall hosted by Barclays Bank. Shops in the mall include Campus Travel, Blackwells Bookshop, Argos, Sainsbury's, Toys 'R' Us, Car Shop, and Eurostar. You can browse through catalogues, and order products for delivery throughout the UK.

BritNet
http://www.britnet.co.uk/
A Web guide to Britain's commercial Web sites. Sites are listed by categories, such as property, cars, information technology, travel and tourism, financial and legal, etc. A valuable starting point for UK services.

Digital Realms
http://www.drealms.co.uk/welcome.html
Another guide to commercial enterprises in the UK that have a presence on the Web. Sites are listed by service and product type.

High Street Directory
http://www.highstreet.com/
A useful guide to businesses and services on the UK Internet.

South Coast Scene
http://prinny.pavilion.co.uk/SouthCoastScene/
A Web site for shops, restaurants, and many other businesses in

the SE of England, many in and around Brighton.

The Shopping Pavilion
http://www.vossnet.co.uk/shopping/
A guide to some of the UK's major retail Web sites, from the commercial Internet and Web service provider, Voss Net.

The UK Shopping Centre
http://www.ukshops.co.uk:8000/
At the moment there are only a few Internet 'shops' at this site, but the number will undoubtedly increase. The stated aim of the site is to counterbalance the bias towards American virtual shopping malls on the Internet! All the shops are categorised and indexed. The UK Shopping Centre has 180,000 books, 56,000 videos, 14,000 CDs, plus computer software, PC games, CD-ROMs, jewellery, gifts, and sports gear.

UK Business on the Web
http://www.u-net.com/ukcom/
A guide to a variety of businesses in the UK that have a presence on the Web. There are over 300 entries in the database. Entries may be listed alphabetically, or by subject categories, which include: advice and services, computing, employment, financial, food and drink, internet, industrial, media, property, retail and travel.

UK Commercial Sites
http://src.doc.ic.ac.uk/uk-commercial.html
A listing of links to commercial Web sites in the UK, compiled by Imperial College, London.

Employment Services
The advent of the Web has meant that for many jobseekers, there is no longer a need to trail around recruitment agencies, or wade through newpaper advertisements. The Internet provides an obvious link between employers and potential employees, when both parties are users. There are a number of Web sites that provide information on employment opportunities in the UK and abroad, and others which allow you to post your CV.

CVWeb
http://cvweb.aston.ac.uk/
An employment service offered by Aston University, which enables jobseekers to place their CVs on the Web, for potential employers to read. Text, images, sound and video can be included in CVs. The service is particularly aimed at students seeking jobs. There are also links to UK university careers services which have Web sites, links to many company Web pages that contain job advertisements, and links to UK and international recruitment agencies.

JobServe
http://www.jobserve.com/
A UK-based service for jobs in information technology (IT). IT recruitment agencies send their latest requirements to JobServe, who sort and collate the information, and place it on a database. You can search the database from these Web pages. Typically there are more than a thousand vacancies, from more than a hundred agencies, in the JobServe Database. Alternatively, you can subscribe to the JobServe e-mail list, which means that you will get a list of new vacancies e-mailed to you every day. The e-mailed job listings may be filtered according to your requirements. Subscription to the service is free.

PeopleBank
http://www.peoplebank.co.uk/ten/
PeopleBank is a free job finding service. Candidates may post their CVs on the PeopleBank database via the Internet. The database is searched by over six thousand clients outside the Internet. Adverts are also posted regularly for vacancies. Candidates may retain their confidentiality if desired.

Reed Jobnet
http://www.reed.co.uk/
This is a Web service provided by Reed Personnel Services, the largest employment agency group in the UK, with over two hundred high-street branches. They offer a wide range of specialist recruitment divisions, including international recruitment. Some of their departments/employment areas which may be accessed via the Web include computing, graduate employment, accountancy, insurance, catering, drivers, technical,

nursing, paramedic, management, training and charity. There are facilities for both employers and jobseekers to register their requirements, and to search through the on-line databases.

The Times Higher Education Supplement
http://www.times.higher.newsint.co.uk/
A Web site providing news, views and world wide jobs in higher education and research. The service is called THESIS (Times Higher Education Supplement Internet Service). Headlines and summaries are updated every Friday, and job advertisements every Tuesday. Also, there are events and promotions listings, book review listings, and a databank containing various information, such as the results of research and teaching surveys in British universities.

UK Commercial Listing - Jobs
http://www.drealms.co.uk/uklist/jobs.html
A service provided by Digital Realms, this Web page provides an extensive listing of links to mainstream recruitment agencies and other Web employment services.

Chapter 6

INFORMATION RESOURCES

Universities, Colleges and Schools

There are very few universities in the developed world that are not yet connected to the Internet. In the UK, not only do most universities have Web servers, so do many colleges and other higher education institutions. They are so numerous, that we are not able to list all of them, but simply give some pointers. More and more schools are also using the Internet, and there are now a large number of educational resources on the Internet, suitable for school children. Some schools also maintain their own Web servers.

City Technology Colleges Trust
http://www.rmplc.co.uk/eduweb/sites/ctctrust/index.html
A guide to the CTC Trust schools and colleges in England, New Zealand, Germany and the United States. Addresses and other contact details are given, including e-mail addresses.

EduWeb
http://www.rmplc.co.uk/eduweb/eduweb.html
A source and guide to educational Web resources for British schools and colleges. There are lists of all the UK's primary and secondary schools, and colleges, that have Web servers, together with some other educational organisations in the UK, such as local education authorities (LEAs). Sites are listed by area, and alphabetically. There are also links to college and school Internet projects. The school and college Web pages, which may be reached from this site, include: information on curricula, including lessons, topics and projects; brochures providing information and pictures of the school or college, its location, and the courses offered; and, material produced by the students.

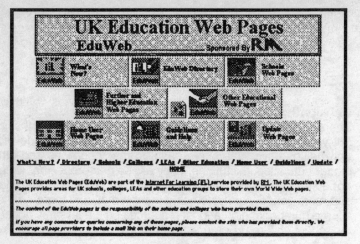

EduWeb

UK Academic Sites
http://src.doc.ic.ac.uk/uk-academic.html
A Web page maintained by Imperial College, London, which provides a long list of links to major UK academic Web sites, which are mostly universities. The institutions are listed in alphabetical order. For many of the institutions, the Web pages for individual departments are also given.

Libraries
For some years now, many libraries, particularly larger university libraries, have been keeping their book catalogues and other archives on computer databases. Librarians and readers in such libraries are able to access the database via computer terminals scattered around the library. As universities (and other large institutions with libraries) installed their own LANs, it was an obvious step to connect their library computers to the LANs, so that staff and students could access the catalogues from anywhere in the university. As the Internet became increasingly popular, library computers were connected to it, so that the public could query the catalogues from anywhere in the world. Today, very many libraries are connected to the Internet, and are said to be 'on-line'. Connection is often via the Telnet or Gopher

Internet methods, which most Web browsers can automatically handle. Increasingly, libraries are providing full Web services and catalogue access.

Library WWW Servers
http://www.lib.washington.edu/~tdowling/libweb.html
A source of links to public and university libraries world wide, which provide Web services. Libraries are listed by country.

Public Libraries with Internet Services
http://www.halcyon.com:80/treasure/library.html
A very comprehensive list of links to public libraries around the world (though with a definite US bias). The libraries are listed by type of Internet service, i.e. Telnet, Gopher, or Web, and then alphabetically.

UK Higher Education Library Catalogues (OPACs)
http://www.niss.ac.uk/reference/opacs.html
A comprehensive list of links to on-line British university library catalogues. The libraries are listed by area and alphabetically.

UK Public Libraries Page
http://dspace.dial.pipex.com/town/square/ac940/ukpublib.html
A very useful starting point for anyone interested in finding on-line public libraries in the UK. There are also many other links to library resources here, many of which will be of particular interest to librarians, such as professional associations, courses, magazines, and information on cataloguing systems.

Encyclopaedias, Dictionaries and Thesauri
Encyclopaedias, dictionaries and thesauri come in book-form, on CD-ROMs, and are now available via the Web. As a means of providing an encyclopaedia, dictionary or thesaurus, the Web has major advantages over other media. The size need not be limited by the data storage capacity of a CD-ROM, or the dimensions of a book, since the definitions may be stored on special high-capacity hard discs or optical discs, attached to an Internet host workstation or mainframe computer. The references and definitions may also be updated and added-to on a daily basis, if

UK Public Libraries Page

required, unlike a CD-ROM or book. There are already a number of on-line encyclopaedia, dictionary and thesaurus databases available to the public via the Internet. Also on the Web, there are related services, such as technical dictionaries, foreign language dictionaries, and acronym databases.

Britannica Online
http://www.eb.com/
This is a Web service provided by the producers of Encyclopedia Britannica. Britannica Online contains more than 65,000 articles from Encyclopedia Britannica's database, including articles and other features not in the print edition. There is a free demonstration you can try, but for full access to the on-line encyclopedia, you must pay a subscription. Some universities and colleges have Britannica Online available to students and staff, via the Web.

Computing Dictionary
http://wombat.doc.ic.ac.uk:80/
A searchable on-line dictionary of acronyms, jargon, programming languages, tools, architecture, operating systems, networking, theory, conventions, standards, mathematics, telecommunications, electronics, institutions, companies,

projects, products, and in fact, anything to do with computing. Simply enter your search word(s) into the form, and a definition will be returned to you. There are more than 8,000 definitions, which are cross-referenced with hypertext links.

French – English Dictionary
http://mlab-power3.uiah.fi/EnglishFrench/avenues.html
Using this service you can translate English words to French, and vice versa. Fast searches can be made by entering one or more words, or part-words, to translate. Searches may return more than one match. You can also look for words associated with your match, and can control whether slang words are returned. Alternatively, you can find words by working your way down a subject tree. This takes longer, but if you have the time, can be very rewarding. There is also a facility which enables you to test your vocabulary.

Hypertext Webster Interface
http://c.gp.cs.cmu.edu:5103/prog/webster
This Web service provides a way of searching Webster's English Dictionary via the Internet. The service is very simple and easy to use. Just type your word into the form, and submit your request. The full dictionary definition of the word will be returned to you. The words in the dictionary definition provide links to further definitions.

Japanese – English Dictionary
http://www.wg.omron.co.jp/cgi-bin/j-e
This service privides English to Japanese translation, and vice versa. You do not need special Japanese fonts installed on your computer, in order to be able to use this service, although if you do, it can take advantage of them.

Pedro's Dictionaries
http://www.public.iastate.edu/~pedro/dictionaries.html
A collection of links to a variety of technical, specialist and language dictionaries on the Web, including Esperanto, Estonian, Finnish, French, German, Hungarian, Italian, Latin, Japanese, Norwegian, Slovak, Slovene, Spanish, Swedish, Russian, Urdu, and Vietnamese.

Roget's Thesaurus
http://web.cs.city.ac.uk/text/roget/thesaurus.html
This Web server allows you to search a public domain version of Roget's Thesaurus, made available by Project Gutenburg. It is in fact Roget's Thesaurus No. 2, derived from the version of Roget's Thesaurus published in 1911. You can either search the entire text of the thesaurus for a particular word, or you can search only the headwords. All entries against each headword are cross-referenced using hypertext links. If so desired, you may download a full list of all the headwords.

Spanish – English Dictionary
http://www.willamette.edu/~tjones/forms/spanish.html
http://www.willamette.edu/~tjones/forms/span2eng.html
These two Web pages provide English to Spanish translation, and Spanish to English translation, respectively. At present the size of the dictionary is quite small, but no doubt will be increased in the future.

World Wide Web Acronym and Abbreviation Server
http://curia.ucc.ie/info/net/acronyms/acro.html
This Web site provides access to a database of acronyms and abbreviations. You can search for an acronym and see its expansion; search for a word in the expansions and see the related acronyms; or, submit an acronym for inclusion in the database. The server records acronyms not found and you can see a list of them. If you happen to know what any mean, you may submit their meanings for inclusion. The database is updated approximately weekly with the additions.

Science and Technology
Since the Internet and the Web were founded and developed by scientists and technologists, it is perhaps not surprising that there are probably more Web sites devoted to these two subjects than any others. In this section we provide a semi-representative, but nevertheless tiny, sample of some of the many thousands of science and technology Web sites now on-line.

Biosciences

http://golgi.harvard.edu/biopages/all.html

An excellent starting point for anyone interested in the biological sciences, with many links to important bioscience Web servers. Links to resources are categorised by subjects, which include agriculture, biochemistry, molecular biology, biophysics, biodiversity and ecology, biotechnology, entomology, evolution, fish and other aquatic animals, developmental biology, forestry, genetics, herpetology (reptiles and amphibians), immunology, medicine, an anaesthesiology, epidemiology, pharmacy, veterinary medicine, microbiology & virology, mycology (fungi), yeasts, neurobiology, and plant biology. There are also links to Web sites providing instructional resources in biology, and job listings in the biosciences.

Centre for Atmospheric Science

http://www.atm.ch.cam.ac.uk/

As well as providing information about atmospheric science research at Cambridge University, this site has many links to meteorology Web servers in the UK. There are also links to current satellite images of UK and European weather systems.

European Space Information System (ESIS)

http://www.esrin.esa.it/htdocs/esis/esis.html

Information here for space scientists, astronomers and astrophysicists. Located at ESRIN, Frascati, Italy in the Information Systems Division of the European Space Agency (ESA), the ESIS project is a service to the space science community to provide access to scientific data, including catalogues, images, spectra and time series from a wide range of ESA/non-ESA space missions. A bibliographic service provides abstracts from a wide range of scientific journals.

Fractal Images

http://www.cnam.fr/fractals.html

An archive of Mandelbrot images and animations, plus links to other sources of information about fractals.

Gateway to Antarctica

http://icair.iac.org.nz/

A guide to all aspects of the Antarctic continent, including its educational value, environmental issues, images, science,

tourism, history, the Antarctic treaty and the latest news about the region.

Global Petroleum Centre
http://www.cadvision.com/oil/
A very complete guide to resources on the Internet for geoscientists, both commercial and academic, involved in the petroleum industry. This site provides lists of, and links to, on-line (and mainstream) geoscience journals, companies, and other Web sources of interest. Also, there is information about professional societies and their Web sites, major events such as conferences, the *sci.geo.petroleum* newsgroup FAQ, plus other *sci.geo* FAQs.

NASA
http://naic.nasa.gov/naic/guide/
For those interested in astronomy and space science, this is an essential guide to all that is available to the public on NASA's computers. There is a lot of scientific data and educational material here. Resources are listed alphabetically, or you can conduct a keyword search.

Natural History Museum
http://www.nhm.ac.uk/
The Natural History Museum in London is dedicated to furthering the understanding of the natural world through its collections, its exhibitions and educational programmes, and through its international programme of scientific research. This server is being developed to provide information on the Museum's exhibitions and public programmes and to provide access to information about the Museum's work and its collections. There are also links from this site to listings of other earth and life science resources on the Internet.

OncoLink – The University of Pennsylvania Cancer Resource
http://cancer.med.upenn.edu/
A major Web site of interest to those involved with cancer research. Here you will find the latest news about cancer research, plus information about various research centres, journals and conferences. The site also acts to collate and disseminate cancer research data.

Physical Sciences, Engineering, Computing and Math – Infomine
http://lib-www.ucr.edu/physci/
A well organised guide to physical science, engineering, computing and mathematics resources on the Internet. Resources can be accessed via an alphabetical listing, or via a keyword search.

The Exploratorium
http://www.exploratorium.edu/
The Exploratorium is located in the Palace Of Fine Arts in the Marina district of San Francisco. It houses a large collection of educational exhibits illustrating contemporary science and technology. The Exploratorium's Web site, styled as 'ExploraNet', is a collection of electronic exhibits and resources for teachers, students, and science and technology enthusiasts. Browsing here is both an educational and a fun experience – highly recommended!

The Met Office
http://www.meto.govt.uk/
Everything you ever wanted to know about the UK Met. Office, and its services, and the science of weather forecasting. In addition, there is the latest forecast for the UK, including the inshore waters forecast, shipping forecast, and gale warnings.

The WEBster: Health Related Sites
http://innet.com/~kathiw/health.html
An alphabetical list of Web sites aimed at individuals looking for information on a variety of health topics, i.e. the health information is consumer-oriented. Here you will find sites containing information on topics as diverse as sleep disorders, HIV/AIDS, cancer, nutrition and alternative medicines.

The WEBster: Medical Sites
http://lucky.innet.com/~kathiw/medical.html
An alphabetical list of medical Web sites of interest to physicians, nurses and other health care professionals. Sites include other medical site catalogues, medical schools, hospitals, professional associations, and medical libraries.

The World Wide Web Virtual Library: Chemistry
http://www.chem.ucla.edu/chempointers.html
A very good starting point for anyone interested in chemistry. There are links here to university chemistry departments, commercial and non-commercial chemistry research organisations, conference announcements, on-line journals, and jobs in the discipline. Chemistry Web sites are listed by country and also alphabetically. Links to chemistry anonymous FTP archive sites are also given.

WebElements
http://www2.shef.ac.uk/chemistry/web-elements/periodic-table.html
WebElements is a 30 megabyte collection of 5,500 files about the periodic table. There is a tremendous amount of data here, much of it in tabular form. The database is constantly being updated.

Arts and Humanities
It is pleasing to see that although the Internet and the Web were developed by scientists and technologists, there are now a large number of Web sites offering arts and humanities resources. Many of these sites are aimed at academics and students, whether at school or university level, but as the Web is increasingly used for leisure, many of these sites are simply there to be enjoyed.

ANU Art History
http://rubens.anu.edu.au/
This server offers access to around 16,000 images, all concerned in some way with the history of art and architecture in the Mediterranean region.

ArtSource
http://www.uky.edu/Artsource/artsourcehome.html
ArtSource is a collection of Internet resources on art and architecture. The content is diverse and includes pointers to resources around the Internet as well as original materials submitted by librarians, artists, and art historians, etc. The site is intended to be selective, rather than comprehensive.

Classics and Mediterranean Archeology
http://rome.classics.lsa.umich.edu/welcome.html

This page provides a vast collection of links to Internet resources, of interest to classicists and Mediterranean archaeologists. There is a built-in search engine to help you find the information that you want.

Fine Art Forum
http://www.msstate.edu/Fineart_Online/home.html

FineArt Forum is a electronic news service that covers art and technology. It is available in three formats: a monthly e-mail digest; an on-line Gopher database and; a fully interactive colour version on the Web. Services include a monthly electronic magazine about art, an image gallery, and links to other art sites.

Internet Poetry Archive
http://sunsite.unc.edu/dykki/poetry/home.html

This archive provides access to selected poems from a number of contemporary poets, such as Seamus Heaney and the Nobel Prize winner in poetry, Czeslaw Milosz. The aim of this site is to make poetry accessible to new audiences and to give teachers and students of poetry new ways of presenting and studying poets and their texts. Each archive entry contains audio clips of the poet reading several poems, the poet's comments on the works, a photograph of the poet and any other graphics that might help a reader understand the poem (e.g., a map or illustration of a particular place mentioned in the poem), texts of the poems, a 500-word critical biography of the poet prepared by a scholar familiar with the poet's work, and a short bibliography. Poems are presented in their original languages, as well as in English translation.

Leeds University Department of Music
http://www.leeds.ac.uk/music.html

Not only a source of information about music at Leeds University, but also a very good source of information about current concerts and other musical events in the UK. Music resources on the Web are listed by artist, genre, instrument, period, and area of origin; as well as by departments and institutions, record companies, and mailing lists. There are also links to information sources on music teaching software.

Oriental Institute
http://www-oi.uchicago.edu/

The Oriental Institute is a museum and research organization, founded in 1919, devoted to the study of the ancient Near East (mainly Egypt and Mesopotamia). This Web site contains images and other information about the relics and art held at the institute, as well as other resources on the history, philology, and archaeology of the Near East.

The Complete Works of Shakespeare
http://the-tech.mit.edu/Shakespeare.html

Here you will find the complete texts for all of William Shakespeare's plays and poems. The works are arranged alphabetically, and also in the order it is believed they were written. You can search all the texts for keywords or phrases. There are also links to other sites with information about the great bard and his works.

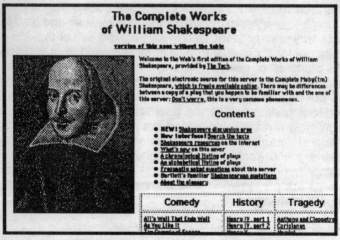

The Complete Works of Shakespeare

The Electric Gallery
http://www.egallery.com/egallery/homepage.html

An impressive collection of images of paintings. Themes include American Indian art, jazz and blues, Haitian, Amazonian, folk art, and contemporary art. Many of the painters exhibiting here hang

in prestigious galleries and museums. Most of the paintings are available for purchase, each of them is unique and original, and orders can be placed via a Web page form or via the phone.

The Electronic Text Center
http://www.lib.virginia.edu/etext/ETC.html
The Electronic Text Center at the University of Virginia provides an on-line archive of thousands of electronic texts, many of which are publicly available. The bulk of the publicly accessible holdings are in the English language, with a few others in French and German. This site also provides links to many other literary resources on the Internet.

The World Wide Web Virtual Library: History
http://kufacts.cc.ukans.edu/history/WWW_history_main.html
A starting point for anyone interested in history and wanting history resources on the Web. Resources are listed by antiquity, by parts of the world, by subject and alphabetically. There are links to information on history conferences, discussion groups, and libraries.

WebMuseum
http://sunsite.doc.ic.ac.uk/wm/
A collection of art images from Paris, together with information about the city itself. Current exhibitions which may be viewed via the Web include one on 20th Century art and one on medieval art. There is a special exhibition of over 100 works by Paul Cezanne, and a selection of works by other famous artists. There is also a small, but interesting collection of classical audio files, including works by Bach, Beethoven and Strauss.

World Wide Arts Resources
http://www.concourse.com/wwar/institut.html
A long list of links to arts and humanities Web sites world wide, including several in the UK.

Governments
More and more national and local government bodies, and agencies, are discovering the benefits of making information publicly available via the Web. Setting-up and maintaining a Web site is

generally a lot cheaper than publication and distribution of conventional reports, manifestos, leaflets and flyers, or providing phone-in 'help' lines, or answering written correspondence. Also, it means that anyone with access to the Web can find information, at any time of day or night, in as great or as little detail as they wish.

Government Centre for Information Systems (CCTA)
http://www.open.gov.uk/index.htm
This Web site provides access to a plethora of information about UK local and national government. There are links to local council Web sites, government ministries, and civil service organisations. The pages are categorised by organisation type: central government departments, agencies, local authorities, and other public bodies. Alternatively, you can look up information by subject or function. There is also a keyword search facility. The site is well organised, and there is a very useful help page, which explains the various facilities available, such as downloadable files, and sending feedback via e-mail.

Government Servers
http://www.eff.org/govt.html
Here you will find an extremely comprehensive list of links to national and local government Web servers world wide, organised on a country by country basis, in alphabetical order. The list of links for the UK is extensive, including links to most regional councils, as well as central government bodies. There are also many links to the European Union Web sites. The list for the US also is particularly exhaustive, including federal government Web sites, and sites listed on a state by state basis.

International Organisations
Many international organisations, such as intergovernmental organisations, political groups, charities and pressure groups are providing information about themselves on the Web, including their objectives, their motives, and their services. Many of these Web pages provide information about membership and making donations also.

Amnesty International
http://www.traveller.com/~hrweb/ai/ai.html
Founded in 1961, Amnesty International is the world's leading human rights organization. This site provides a detailed history of the movement, together with information about its current initiatives. You can find the contact details of Amnesty International in different countries, and there is also information about how to join the organization.

Greenpeace International
http://www.greenpeace.org/
Greenpeace is an independent, campaigning organisation which works to expose global environmental problems, and to force those involved to implement solutions. This site provides information about the organisation's history, its current campaigns, its national centres, and details of how to join and make donations. Other material on offer includes images, press releases, publications, and information about the Greenpeace ships. You can also send feedback via e-mail. There is a list of links to other Web sites of interest to environmentalists.

North Atlantic Treaty Organisation (NATO)
http://www.saclant.nato.int/nato.html
The North Atlantic Treaty, signed in Washington on 4 April 1949, created an alliance for collective defence as defined in Article 51 of the United Nations Charter. The Alliance links fourteen European countries with the United States and Canada. This Web site provides information about NATO and the member countries.

OneWorld Online
http://www.oneworld.org/index.html
A Web home site for a variety of major international charitable and educational organisations. The many links include Amnesty International, Christian Aid, Overseas Development Administration, Oxfam, Save the Children, United Nations Childrens Fund, and the Voluntary Service Organisation. The site offers news items and articles about various global themes and issues, and educational resources for schools.

The European Union
http://www.cec.lu/en/eu.html

A source of information about the European Union (EU), including its history, constitution, the 15 member states, its flag, anthem and currency. There is a keyword search facility, and an interesting FAQ about the EU.

The Red Cross
http://www.icrc.ch/

This is the home page of the International Committee of the Red Cross (ICRC), the international emergency relief agency, based in Geneva, famous for its humanitarian work in war zones. Information is provided here about all ICRC operations, including country maps, facts and figures, reports, news releases, international conferences, and publications on the countries (over 50) in which the ICRC is currently active. There are articles on various issues and topics, such as anti-personnel mines, and blinding weapons, etc. There is information about international humanitarian law – what it is, the texts, their application and analysis, together with a special section for armed forces, and information on the ICRC's CD-ROM on international humanitarian law. In addition, there is information about printed publications, audiovisual and multimedia products available from the ICRC.

United Nations
http://www.un.org/

This is the Web site of the United Nations, the world's leading inter-governmental co-operation organisation. Here you will find the UN charter, and other information about the history of the UN, UN agencies, the Secretaries-General, member states, etc. Selected Documents from the Secretary-General, General Assembly, Security Council, and Economic and Social Council are available for public reading. There is information about UN libraries, international conferences, employment prospects, publicity material, and images from the UN archives. Currently there is a special feature on the 50th anniversary celebration of the UN's foundation.

United Nations

Chapter 7

ENTERTAINMENT AND LEISURE

News

Major newspaper publishers and news networks are now placing reports on the Web, often updated on a daily basis. Some of these services are merely 'samplers' intended to entice you to buy the printed version, whereas others are more comprehensive. Whilst the articles may be briefer than in the printed form, these news services are generally free for anyone to use. Some of these news services also carry weather forecasts.

Although free, some of these news services require that you firstly fill out a Web 'registration' form and submit it to the news service Web server. You may be required to enter your name and address, and other personal details, together with a user name and password of your choice. When choosing a password, do not use one that you already use for more secure applications, such as logging-in to a network at work, or a BBS. Whilst the services listed here are reputable, there is no guarantee that your chosen password will not be intercepted by a third party and used unscrupulously. Once you have registered and have full access to a news service, create a 'bookmark' for the main news index page, so that each subsequent time you access the news service, you do not need to re-enter your user name and password.

CNN Interactive
http://www.cnn.com/
A first class on-line news service from the US, but with plenty of international news. The articles make particularly good use of images and video clips. Regular departments include US news, world news, business, sports, showbusiness, weather, politics, technology, food and health, and style. Other interesting features include a news quiz, news and reviews of the latest movies to hit the big screen, a video 'vault', and a keyword search facility.

Daily Record and Sunday Mail
http://www.record-mail.co.uk/rm/
Scotland's popular tabloids have arrived on the Web. Departments include news, sport, features, letters, and contests.

FutureNet World News
http://www.futurenet.co.uk/cgi-passwd/passwd_login.pl/News/today/
News reports are updated daily at about 1 pm, and cover both UK and World news. News items are also listed by subjects, including business, court, crime, economy, education, general, health, politics, royal news, show business and transport. There are also comprehensive international sports news pages. Links to back-issue news reports covering the preceding few days can also be accessed. This service requires you to register before you can use it.

Internet Online Newspapers
http://mfginfo.com/htm/newspapers.htm
A very comprehensive list of links to Web news services in countries all around the world, listed on a regional basis.

IPL's News Review
http://www.news-review.co.uk/
An on-line news service which provides a comprehensive summary of the economic, financial and corporate news in twelve of the UK's leading weekend newspapers. News items are indexed by company and newspaper. New issues appear every Tuesday, and cover the preceding weekend. If you wish for more information about subscribing to the paper version, or receiving a customised electronic version by e-mail, complete the form provided.

Reed Regional Newspapers, Lancashire
http://www.reednews.co.uk/
A selection of on-line newspapers covering Lancashire and the northwest of England. As well as news, there are property, motoring and 'what's on' guides for the region.

The Electronic Telegraph
http://www.telegraph.co.uk/
Updated daily, this service provides shortened news articles selected from the Daily Telegraph newspaper. The leading stories appear on the 'Front Page'. UK news is listed under 'Home' news. World news and sport news items are listed separately. Links are used to cross-reference news articles, and are also used to reference earlier news items. There are also longer features on contemporary issues, and a comprehensive business section. The 'Gazette' links you to the daily crossword, cartoons, horoscopes, the weather forecast and to excerpts from The Spectator magazine, together with subscription information. The Electronic Telegraph requires you to register before you use the service, although it is free to use.

The Financial Times
http://www.ft.com/
The Financial Times Web site offers highlights of the daily newspaper, and a guide to other services offered by the Financial Times Group. This Web site provides a digest of business news, marketing news, business opportunities, political and economic news, and also monitors the world media. The site also provides some financial data, including world stock market indices. Details of other financial data services, and how much they cost, are also provided.

The Socialist Worker
http://www.anu.edu.au/polsci/marx/contemp/swuk/swuk.html
This Web site provides an on-line version of current and back issues of Socialist Worker, the official newspaper of the UK Socialist Workers Party. Plenty to read here about contemporary socialism and Marxism. Note that some of the Web documents are very large and may take some while to download.

Times Newspapers
http://www.the-times.co.uk/
This Web site provides access to free Internet editions of The Times, The Sunday Times, and The Times Higher Educational Supplement. The site also provides interactive facilities.

UK Today
http://www.kdtech.co.uk/
UK Today is a news services provided by KD Technology, only available via the Web. UK Today provides a daily summary of the UK's news and sport, together with the pick of the day's top news and sports stories. Daily features include film reviews and previews, and a television column. Also available at this site is a regional on-line newspaper, the Luton & Dunstable Evening Post. KD Technology requires you to register before you use these services, although no user name or password are required.

TV and Radio
Guides to TV and radio programmes are now available on the Web. There are also Web pages dedicated to particular TV shows.

BBC
http://www.bbcnc.org.uk
This is the home Web site of the BBC, and provides a tremendous amount of information about the corporation and its projects, as well as programming guides which cover all BBC TV and radio programmes, both for the UK and the World Service. There are also links to several programmes which have their own home pages, such as Top Gear, Horizon, Tomorrow's World, and Blue Peter.

Channel 4 Programme Support Online
http://www.cityscape.co.uk/channel4/-home.html
This site provides further information about recent and current Channel 4 programmes. You can also order printed booklets and factsheets related to programmes that have been aired.

Nerd World : Television
http://www.tiac.net/users/dstein/nw59.html
A comprehensive list of links to television-related resources on the Web, including programme guides and home pages for particular shows. There is also a list of links to Network News groups for fans of particular shows.

Electronic Magazines

As well as news services on the Web, there are now a huge number of magazines on the Web, often called electronic magazines, or 'e-zines' for short. Some of these are electronic versions or spin-offs of conventional printed publications, whereas others have only ever existed in cyberspace.

Computer Magazines
http://www.asiaonline.net/publicat.htm

Many popular computer magazines found in highstreet newsagents also offer articles and other services via the Internet. This is a list of links to some of the most popular computer magazines on the Web, including Computer Shopper, MacUser, MacWEEK, PC Computing, PC Magazine, PC Week, Windows Magazine and Windows Sources.

Cyberkind
http://sunsite.unc.edu/ckind/title.htm

This Web site offers articles on the Internet, a wide range of short stories and poetry, plus images by contemporary artists.

Cyberzine
http://www.cyberzine.com/

This e-zine, published monthly, features many comic strips, works of contemporary fiction, non-fiction and art. There is a source of links to the latest interesting sites on the Web. Cyberzine also provides a live Internet 'chat' facility. There is a choice of discussion groups, and for each one, there is a list of the currently active members. You can join any group and contribute your comments, all in real time.

Electronic Journals
http://www.physiol.ox.ac.uk/mag.html

A useful list of links to various magazines and newspapers on the Web, many of which are UK based.

Electronic Newsstand
http://enews.com/

A Web site that provides links to articles from the world's leading magazines, newsletters, newspapers, and catalogues. It is also a guide to current news and events, and the latest popular Web

sites. Web pages are categorised, and topics include business, computers and technology, entertainment, automotive, health, politics, travel, sports and recreation, books, news, catalogues and newspapers.

E-Zine List
http://www.meer.net/~johnl/e-zine-list/index.html
John Labovitz's directory of over 600 e-zines around the world, which are accessible via the Web, Gopher, FTP, e-mail, and other services. The list is updated at the beginning of each month.

Magazines Online and E-Zines
http://www.ukdirectory.com/news/mag.htm
A list of links to mainly UK-based magazines that may be reached via the Web, including a number of UK computer magazines that offer on-line facilities.

On-Line Magazines
http://www.middlebury.edu/~otisg/zines.shtml
A very extensive collection of links to e-zines from all around the globe, listed in alphabetical order.

Pathfinder
http://pathfinder.com/
Home to a variety of mostly US-based news and leisure magazines that offer Web services, including Time Magazine, People, Asiaweek, National Review, Money, Fortune, Digital Pulse, Entertainment Weekly, Windows Magazine, NetGuide, Home PC, Sports Illustrated, Time Life, and Vibe. This Web site also offers 'chat' facilities and 'message boards' that enable Internet users to exchange views, and discuss current issues. There is also a powerful search facility, which allows you to do keyword searches on all the magazines at this site.

Planet Science
http://www.newscientist.com/
Planet Science is the Web magazine of New Scientist, the UK-based weekly magazine of popular science. The Web site contains news, features, reviews and comment drawn from each issue of New Scientist, the answers to questions about puzzling

scientific phenomena in everyday life, and contributions from readers.

Private Eye
http://www.intervid.co.uk/intervid/eye/gateway.html
The Web version of one of Britain's most notorious satirical magazines. You will find here all the usual biting commentary on contemporary British politics and society, plus the cartoons, and the regular features, such as Pseuds, Great Bores of Today, Lord Gnome, and Netballs.

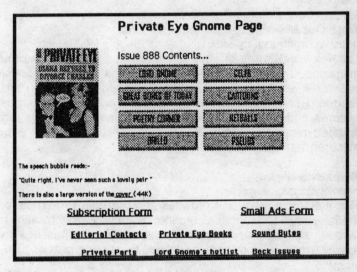

Private Eye

The Economist
http://www.enews.com/magazines/economist/
The Economist magazine offers commentary and analysis on world politics, business, finance, science, technology and the arts. This Web site provides a selection of lengthy articles from the current and recent issues of The Economist magazine, in an effort to entice you to subscribe. Whether you do or do not, these well-written essays are well worth a read.

Time World Wide
http://www.timeinc.com/time/timehomepage.html
Here you will find articles from the latest issue of Time Magazine, which provide in-depth coverage of both US and international news and current affairs. There are special departments dedicated to European and to Asian issues. There are also pages devoted to the latest incoming news stories, and these pages are updated continuously. Also on-line are the Time Magazine letters pages. An interesting feature of this Web site is the 'message board' service, similar to Network News, whereby you can join a variety of topical discussion groups and contribute your views.

Time Out Net
http://www.timeout.co.uk
Time Out Net is the Internet version of the popular Time Out magazine. It offers city guides, and arts and entertainment listings for Amsterdam, Berlin, London, Madrid, New York, Paris, Prague, Rome and San Francisco. There are in-depth reports, features and a free classified advertising service. Listings are updated weekly on Wednesdays. This service is free, but you must register before using it.

Webster's Weekly
http://www.awa.com/w2
This electronic magazine provides short articles by authors on the Internet, which cover all manner of subjects, from politics to humour, and from economics to relationships. Back issues are readily available, and there is no need to pay or register.

HotWired
http://www.hotwired.com
One of the best known electronic magazines, with all sorts of articles and news about the Web, the Internet, and life beyond cyberspace! The production is colourful and very slick, and definitely a product of the 90's. The magazine is interactive, in that there are discussion areas, and you may send e-mail for publication. There are also many interesting links from HotWired to other places on the Web. There is limited access for guests, if you just want to have a look around. If you want to use all the facilities, you must register. At present registration is free.

Sport

There are now a huge number of Web pages devoted to sport. The very latest sports news can usually be found in the various on-line newspapers, described earlier in this chapter, but for more in-depth articles and reports, try the following Web guides.

ElNet Galaxy Sports Page

http://www.einet.net/galaxy/Leisure-and-Recreation/Sports.html
A large variety of sports are listed here, including everything from air hockey to wrestling. Simply follow the link to the sport which interests you. There are also links to individual articles and compendiums of articles, to other sports directories, to sporting organisations on the Web, to the latest sporting events, and to electronic magazines dedicated to sport, such as Alpine World Magazine, SportZwired, Stoked!, and Sports Illustrated.

The WWW Virtual Sports Library

http://www.atm.ch.cam.ac.uk/sports/sports.html
The various sports covered on these pages are grouped in a rather curious manner, but otherwise this is a useful guide to a variety of sports and the latest happenings in the world of sport. Most coverage is given to soccer, perhaps reflecting the British origin of these pages. Also covered are American football, baseball, basketball, Canadian football league, rugby, cricket, hockey, tennis, golf, cycling, motor racing, sailing, surfing, diving, swimming, fishing, skiing, climbing, walking, athletics, and martial arts.

World Wide Web of Sports

http://tns-www.lcs.mit.edu/cgi-bin/sports
Another guide to sport, with sport links listed alphabetically. Dozens of sports are covered, from archery to weight-lifting.

Travel

For every country on the Internet, you will almost always be able to find a Web guide to the country, aimed at visitors and potential visitors. Some of these are run by enthusiastic and patriotic net citizens, whilst many are run by the established tourist boards. As a result, the quality of what you will find is highly variable! Many of these kinds of Web pages are slow to

World Wide Web of Sports

Custom Page   Submit A Link   Sports Search

Archery	Athletic Games	Aussie Rules
Badminton	Ballooning	Baseball
Basketball	Bowling	Boxing
Cheerleading/Music	Chess and Checkers	Climbing
Commercial Sites	Cricket	Curling
Cycling	Dancing	Diving
Equestrian	Fencing	Field Hockey

Fishing	Footbag	Football
Frisbee	Golf	Gymnastics
Hang Gliding	Hand Ball	Hunting
HydroPlaning	Ice Hockey	Jet Skiing
Jump Rope	Kayaking	Korfball
Lacrosse	Martial Arts	Motor Sports
Outdoor Sports	Parlor Games	Paintball
Petanque	Publications	Racquetball

World Wide Web of Sports

download, since they contain images of the countries described, so you may wish to turn off the image downloading facility on your browser. There are also more general guides to travel on the Web, including information about booking accommodation and travel tickets. Many major airlines are now on-line. The following pages are only general pointers to the world of travel.

Airlines of the Web
http://www.haas.berkeley.edu/%7Eseidel/airline.html
An excellent guide to airlines, their routes and timetables around the world. Links to all airlines that offer Web services, of which there are very many, can be found here. This is also a great resource for anyone working in the airline industry.

Australia
http://www.csu.edu.au/education/australia.html
A good starting point for anyone interested in holidaying in Australia. Lots of facts and figures about the country, as well as links to Australian Web sites.

Canada
http://www.cybersmith.net/compuguide/canada/
An excellent starting point for anyone interested in Canada, or travelling there. Plenty of information about its culture, people, government, regions, and national parks.

France
http://www.france.com/francescape/top.html
This Web site provides lots of information about France, and vacations in France. Features include an illustrated tour of the main French regions and cities, general information you need to know when planning a trip to France, lists of tour operators, lists of festivals and events, and transport information.

Germany
http://www.chemie.fu-berlin.de/adressen/brd.html
Information about Germany, including its geography, people, economy, government, and communications. There are also maps and images.

Greece
http://www.vacation.forthnet.gr/index.html
A Web site aimed at tourists planning a holiday to Greece, including copious information about the country, plus many images of Greece. All aspects of holidays in the country are covered.

Hotel Net
http://www.u-net.com/hotelnet/
A guide to hotels in Europe. Search for accommodation by selecting the country, town, and region, either by selecting the text links, or by clicking on the maps. For each hotel there is a photo, copious information about the hotel, including prices. You can send for more information, and make bookings, simply by filling-in and submitting the Web page forms provided.

Hotel UK
http://www.demon.co.uk/hotel-uk/
Information about selected hotels in the UK and Europe, for business travellers and others. Booking details are provided.

Ireland
http://www.bess.tcd.ie/ireland.html
Maps and information about Ireland, including food, language, literature and theatre, music, economics, politics and current affairs. There are also links to other tourist guides to Ireland.

Italy
http://www.emmeti.it/Welcome/
A guide to Italy, including information on selected resorts, tourist attractions, restaurants, monuments, history and culture. A good starting point for anyone interested in the country.

Lonely Planet Publications
http://www.lonelyplanet.com.au/lp.htm
This is the official Web site belonging to the publishers of the popular Lonely Planet guide books, aimed at young and adventurous travellers on a low budget. There are clickable maps and links to condensed, hypertext versions of the guide books, pertaining to a large number of countries all around the world. These include text, maps and pictures. There are also many, many pages of hints and tips contributed by travellers just returned from far-flung parts. You may also send feedback yourself, which may even make it into print in the next edition of the relevant Lonely Planet guide book. Whilst the on-line Lonely Planet guides may not be portable like the printed versions, they are free, and make great reading, before or after you have gone on your travels.

New Zealand
http://nz.com/NZ/
A Web guide to New Zealand, with plenty of facts and figures about the country, images, and links to NZ Web sites.

Spain
http://www.spaintour.com/
An introduction to Spain for tourists, from the Spanish tourist office. This site contains extensive information on towns and provinces of Spain, culture, and history.

The Virtual Tourist II
http://www.xmission.com:80/~kinesava/vt/
The Virtual Tourist II is a map-based guide to the World. It

provides a huge amount of information, of interest to tourists, geographers, and community services. The starting point is a clickable World map. This leads to increasingly detailed regional and local maps, and ultimately to local information and Web servers.

UK Directory - Travel
http://www.ukdirectory.com/travel/travel.htm
This Web resource provides guides to many towns and cities in the UK; information on holidays, tours and special interest activities; hotels, B&B's and other accommodation; tourist attractions in and around the UK; plus information and contact details for British travel agents, guides and tourist boards. Many travel agents and airlines now offer information via the Web, and even on-line booking facilities.

UK Hotel and Guest House Directory
http://www.s-h-systems.co.uk/shs.html
A very comprehensive list of UK accommodation. You can browse by selecting the first letter of the town of your choice, and then selecting the town of your choice from the list. You can also find accommodation using a map, or use the search facility to find an establishment by name. Listings vary in length and detail, but commonly include pictures, ratings, types of accommodation available, tariffs, location and contact details. Users of this Web service can commonly get discounts when booking.

Music and Films
There are now abundant Web sites offering information and reviews of the latest CDs and films to be released, as well as older music and films. These commonly include images, sound and even video clips, which may be accessed provided you have the appropriate software.

Internet Underground Music Archive
http://www.iuma.com/IUMA-2.0/lf-home.html
A showcase on the Web for independent artists from around the world. More than 700 are represented here. Artists may be picked by genre, by name, or by location. Genres include blues, childrens, classical, country, easy listening, country, pop, rock,

punk, and many others. For each artist, there is a description of the artist and their work. Reviews and comments are also available, and you may contribute your own. You may download and play either an excerpt from the artist's work, or the whole thing. Likewise, if there is a video, you can download an excerpt or the whole thing. If you like a particular work, you can order it, using the Web forms provided.

Music Servers
http://musicinfo.gold.ac.uk/index/music.html
A UK-based guide to music resources on the Web, ranging from sound files, to information about concerts and composers.

On-line Digitized Music
http://ftp.luth.se/pub/sounds/songs
This is a very straightforward archive of sound files which you may download and play on your computer. Songs are by popular artists, mainly from the 60's, 70's, 80's and 90's. For example, you will find songs here by artists as diverse as The Beatles, Enya, Pink Floyd, Santana, Guns 'n' Roses, Wham, and The Grateful Dead.

The Internet Movie Database
http://www.cm.cf.ac.uk/Movies/
A well established and extremely comprehensive archive of films, both recent and old. You can search for a film by name, or by using a number of other criteria, such as actors, producers, directors, genre, subject matter, location, etc. For most films, you can find when and where it was made, and by whom, the cast, the production crew, and the plot. Often there are images from the films, and information about associated books, etc. Selecting a person from one of the cast lists returns a list of all the other films they have been involved in. You can then find out more about these films. The database is rich with cross-references. There are also links to film reviews given in major electronic magazines, in Network News, and elsewhere. You can even submit your own personal ratings and reviews for a film, or any other information you can add to the database.

The Mammoth Music Meta List
http://pathfinder.com/vibe/mmm/music.html
This Web server provides a tremendous amount of information,

The Internet Movie Database

categorised by geographical area, artist, recording label, and by instrument. There are lyrics, and reviews. Genres of music in the database include classical and opera, Christian music, country and western, comedy music, folk, film music, rock, alternative, hip hop, jazz and blues, reggae, ska and bhangra, a cappella, Indian music, native American music, Irish music, Russian music, latino/hispanic music, new age, morris dancing, and barbershop quartet. There is also information on radio stations and shows, performances, MIDI and other computer music, music on-line magazines, music festivals, and much else.

Books
The Web has lots to offer for those interested in literature. Bookshops on the Web which offer on-line mail-order facilities may be accessed via some of the commercial pages mentioned

in Chapter 5. Libraries with on-line catalogues may be accessed from some of the Web pages described in Chapter 6.

Here we describe some other literary resources on the Web, and pointers to the many thousands of books and other texts now available directly on the Internet. These books are often called 'on-line books, 'electronic texts' or 'e-texts' for short. They are free, and may be read on-line, or downloaded to your computer and read later. On-line books are generally classic novels and other works of literature, for which the copyright has expired, so that they are effectively in the 'public domain'. A few e-texts are more recent works which have not been published in the printed form, and are only available via the Internet.

Children's Literature Web Guide
http://www.ucalgary.ca/%7Edkbrown/
This Web resource is an attempt to gather together and categorize the growing number of Internet resources related to books for children and young adults. Most of the information that you can find through these pages is provided by schools, libraries, and commercial enterprises involved in the book world. The kind of information you can find here includes the results of the latest book awards, links to booksellers and publishers on the Web, educational resources, and information about films based on children's books. There are a lot of stories available on the Internet to read or download. Some of them are from well-known books, others can be found only on-line. This site provides pointers to these on-line children's books.

Internet Book Information Center
http://sunsite.unc.edu/ibic/IBIC-homepage.html
This site provides hundreds of links to literary resources on the Web. There is information about on-line books, as well as more conventional publications. This site will be of interest to readers, writers and publishers alike.

Project Gutenberg
http://jg.cso.uiuc.edu/pg/
The aim of Project Gutenberg is to create on-line versions of as many non-copyrighted texts as possible. To their credit, they have already managed to create a formidable archive / library of on-line texts, all of which may be accessed from this Web site for

free. You may either read them on-line, or download them to read later. Texts include many classic works, by authors such as Robert Louis Stevenson, Arthur Conan Doyle, Edgar Rice Burroughs, Rudyard Kipling, Mark Twain, and Geoffrey Chaucer.

The On-line Books Page
http://www.cs.cmu.edu/Web/books.html
Look here for an index of over one thousand on-line books, and for common repositories of on-line books and other documents. Searches may be done using either author name or title. There is also a subject listing and a 'new' books listing. There are also many other links to literary resources, booksellers, etc. Of especial interest are the links to repositories of foreign and classical language e-texts.

Games
There are many Web sites catering for games enthusists. In Chapter 4, we described some of the main software archives on the Internet. Freeware and shareware computer games for PCs and Macintoshes can be downloaded from these sites. In this section, as well as pointers to downloadable game software, we describe some other resources for gamers. For instance, there are many Web sites aimed at fans of specific commercial PC and Macintosh games. There are also many sites dedicated to players of more conventional games, such as bridge and chess. Some sites provide multi-player games, in which each player is connected via the Internet. Some of these aim to create a virtual reality for the players in cyberspace. As the Internet becomes more sophisticated, so will the games that are possible.

Cardiff Video Game Database Browser
http://www.cm.cf.ac.uk/Games
A Web site aimed at fans of video games. You will find here hints, tips, reviews and other information pertaining to the major types of video games, including Sega, Nintendo, Amiga, Atari, 3DO and CD-i.

Chess Space
http://www.redweb.com/chess/
A well organised guide to chess resources on the Web. Of particular interest are the links to on-line chess sites, where you may play other people on the Internet in real time, such as the Internet Chess Club (telnet://chess.lm.com:5000).

Computer Draughts and Checkers Page
http://carol.fwi.uva.nl/~grimmink/draughts.html
An excellent resource on everything to do with the games of draughts and checkers. The site includes information on the rules, problems, players, tournaments, commercial computer versions of the games, plus downloadable freeware and shareware.

Games Domain
http://www.gamesdomain.co.uk/
The premier UK gaming resource on the Web, this site provides a tremendous amount of information about all types of games, including computer games, non-computer games, and Internet games. A useful feature is the search facility, which allows you to root out information about a game, simply by entering its name. Other features include an electronic magazine called The GD Review, competitions, and information for programmers. There is an excellent facility for downloading freeware and shareware games, demos and patches for both PCs and Macintoshes. There are also many pointers to other key Web gaming sites, including hundreds of links to game playing FAQs, anonymous FTP sites, games home pages, electronic magazines, and commercial sites. Topics include everything from Doom to Darts, and MUDs to Mortal Kombat.

Internet Chess Library
http://www.onenet.net/chess/
A major archive of information about the game of chess, including players, past and present tournaments, and games.

Internet Gaming Zone
http://www.zone.com/
Here, you can play 'hearts', 'bridge', 'chess', and 'go', with other people, live on the Internet. In order to use the service, you must

firstly download the free software, available for Macintoshes and PCs. This provides a full graphical games interface for whichever game you wish to play. Further games will be added to this service soon.

Puzzle Archives
http://www.nova.edu/Inter-Links/puzzles.html
This Web sites provides access to puzzles and brain teasers archived from the newsgroups recently published puzzles which are categorized by subject. Both the puzzles and their solutions are given.

Stephen's WWW Backgammon
http://www.statslab.cam.ac.uk/~sret1/backgammon/main.html
A key Web site for those interested in the game of backgammon. It provides many links to popular backgammon resources on the Internet. Topics covered here include the basic rules, playing backgammon on the Internet, backgammon computer programs, books and magazines, matches, clubs and competitions.

The Game Cabinet
http://www.gamecabinet.com/
The Game Cabinet Web site provides rules, rule variants, reviews and other miscellaneous information about board games from around the world. Some of the articles were written for the Game Cabinet and others have been culled from the Internet. The Game Cabinet covers mainly family and strategy games.

The WorldWideWeb Bridge Directory
http://rgb.anu.edu.au/Bridge/WWW-Bridge.html
A guide to the card game of bridge, with links to a large number of bridge resources on the Internet. There are links to live Internet bridge games, in which you may partake.

UK National Lottery
http://www.connect.org.uk/lottery/
Here you will find everything you need to know about the UK National Lottery, including perhaps the most important piece of information – the latest winning numbers!

Chapter 8

WEB BROWSERS

Netscape Navigator

Netscape Navigator, commonly known simply as *Netscape*, is currently the most popular Web browser amongst PC and Macintosh users. The browser's origins can be traced back to the NCSA (National Center for Supercomputing Applications), at the University of Illinois, which developed the *Mosaic* browser (described below). The NCSA still produces *Mosaic*, and there are also several commercial versions of *Mosaic*. However, the success of Mosaic has been eclipsed by *Netscape*. In March 1994, Marc Andreessen and several colleagues who had worked on the development of *Mosaic* left NCSA for a new company, Netscape Communications Corporation, with the aim of developing their own superior version of *Mosaic*. The first public release of the software, called *Netscape Navigator*, came in November 1994.

The software is provided as freeware for educational institutions and other non-profit making organisations, and hence has become very popular. It is difficult to be certain what proportion of those surfing the Web use *Netscape*. There are several pages on the Web that purport to measure the statistics of browser usage accurately. Perusal of these pages indicates that *Netscape* is almost definitely the most popular browser, although by how much is arguable. Perhaps one of the more reliable estimates comes from the popular 'Yahoo' site (see Chapter 4). The data collected indicates that currently about 70% of those using the Web use *Netscape*.

For commercial users the software is not free, and hence Netscape Communications are able to make a profit from selling commercial licences. Many large companies and other institutions are adopting *Netscape* as their official browser. For example, in July 1995, Hewlett Packard provided *Netscape* for all its employees. Netscape Communications also sell Web server software and other services. The success of *Netscape* led

to the flotation of the company on the US stock market in August 1995. Share values more than doubled within minutes of the launch!

Netscape is available for both *Windows* and Macintosh machines. At the time of writing, the latest official release was version 1.1, with version 2 at the beta testing stage. Like other browsers, *Netscape* is available for downloading from anonymous FTP archives on the Internet, from LAN administrators, from computer clubs, and from Netscape Communications itself. The company's address and URLs are given in Appendix 2.

The browser has a lot of favourable attributes. Although it is free to the majority of users, its design is slick and professional. Installation is easily achieved using the installer program, which automatically places the necessary files and directories on your computer's hard disc, and configures the program to work with your particular system. When you start the program, it automatically connects to Netscape Communications' computers in the USA, and the *Netscape* welcome page. From this page there are links to a variety of useful Web resources, and good jumping-off points for exploration of the Web, but more importantly, there is an excellent on-line help facility. Everything you need to know about the operation of the program is here, written in a concise and clear manner. Hypertext links lead you quickly from topic to topic, and from question to answer. Experienced and novice *Netscape* users alike will find the on-line help a real treasure trove of information about their browser.

Netscape can be easily configured to use a variety of helper applications. However, it already has in-built capabilities for downloading and displaying both GIF and JPEG images, so there is no real need to have a graphic images helper program. Interlaced images are utilised, which means that images can be displayed gradually whilst downloading is taking place. Whilst downloading Web pages or other files, progress is shown at the bottom of the screen. If you decide you want to stop downloading a page, this is easily done at any stage. Simply press the 'Stop' button, or select another Web page link instead. You can also have several Web pages open simultaneously, simply by opening extra *Netscape* windows for each Web document.

Browser functions can be selected from a pull-down menu bar at the top of the screen display, which is logically laid out. Some functions are also available using the row of buttons beneath the

menu bar. For example, Web pages may be reviewed quickly and easily by using the 'back' and 'forward' arrows, or the history list. Favourite Web pages may be added to a bookmark list, which itself can be subdivided and grouped in a hierarchical manner. There are useful facilities for editing the bookmark list. Items on the bookmark list may be quickly selected using pull-down menus.

In addition, there is a very usable newsreader program, which allows you to read and contribute to Network News, and respond to other posters. You can also browse all the newsgroups available from your local newsfeed, and choose which you wish to subscribe to.

You can also send e-mail using *Netscape*, including the text from Web pages or Network News articles in your messages if you wish, and other files as attachments. However, you can not receive e-mail.

The browser is also able to offer secure connections to Web sites that use the SSL method, which means that it is ideal for anyone who wishes to use the Web for financial transactions, or transfer of other sensitive information.

Perhaps most importantly, *Netscape* is, in general, very stable, i.e. it does not hang-up or crash too often, something that Internet applications are not generally renowned for!

NCSA Mosaic

The web browser *Mosaic* from the NCSA (National Center for Supercomputing Applications) has also been extremely successful since it was released in 1993, and only relatively recently has it been overtaken in popularity by programs such as *Netscape*. *Mosaic* was the very first browser to become available for both Macintoshes and PCs. Since then it has undergone much development, and many of the early problems with the software have been eradicated, although it still has more bugs and less flexibility than more recently developed browsers such as *Netscape*.

The latest version of NCSA *Mosaic* is available for Microsoft *Windows, Windows for Workgroups, Windows NT*, and *OS/2 Warp*, as well as Macintoshes. NCSA *Mosaic* is freeware and available from NCSA, as well as many other Internet software archives, via anonymous FTP. Installation is quite simple. NCSA *Mosaic* has a number of user-friendly features. For example,

when you move the cursor over the control buttons on-screen, the help system explains their functions. As you download Web pages and other documents, the size of the document is shown, as well as how much has been downloaded. You can mark your favourite Web pages, such that they either appear in a 'hotlist', or at the bottom of the screen, so you can quickly re-select them. You can also add URLs to the pull-down menus, which provides another way of accessing often used pages.

On the negative side, although NCSA *Mosaic* allows you to read newsgroups, there is no facility for managing a list of your favourite ones, nor can you send articles to newsgroups. Neither is there e-mail support. There are also still a few bugs, particularly associated with printing Web pages, and using the print preview facility. Security features are not very advanced with this version of *Mosaic*.

The success of NCSA *Mosaic* has spawned several commercial spin-offs, with subtly different features and improvements. These products began arriving on the market in mid-1994, and have attracted as much, or more interest as the original product. *Netscape*, described earlier, is the most popular spin-off. Some of the others are described below.

Spry Air Mosaic

Spry *Air Mosaic* from Spry Incorporated is fully commercial, although a demo is available for free. It was developed from the original NCSA *Mosaic*, and requires *OS/2 Warp* or *Windows*.

Spry *Air Mosaic* has a number of key features. It increases the viewing speed of Web pages by loading text first, enabling the user to scroll and read the page whilst images are updated, a method also employed within *Netscape*. An unusual browser feature is the ability to 'switch off' the menu bar temporarily, which enables you to see more of a Web page at one time. This is the so-called 'Kiosk' mode. Whilst in 'Kiosk' mode, you can select links and download other documents, but you lose the other browser facilities. URLs can be easily added to a 'hotlist', and retrieved using the 'hotkey'. URLs may also be sorted into folders, and selected from a pull-down menu. You may create up to 15 folders, with 200 URLs in each. Spry *Air Mosaic* also provides for Telnet, FTP and Gopher connections. There is a limited newsreader and support for sending e-mail.

Spry *Air Mosaic* is also incorporated in *NetLauncher*, a product available to CompuServe customers, enabling exploration of the Web via the CompuServe BBS.

Spyglass Enhanced Mosaic

Spyglass *Mosaic* was the first commercial version of the NCSA original, and there are versions for both Macintoshes and PCs.

Spyglass *Mosaic* offers some improvements over the original NCSA *Mosaic*, although the *Windows* version still has a few bugs. The printing facility, in particular, is much improved. There is support for forms, and also for having several windows open at once. The latter is particularly useful, allowing you to have several Web pages open at once. When downloading a document, it is possible to abort the download by pressing the 'escape' key, which is useful if the download process is taking too long. There is a newsreader facility with limited capabilities. The browser has built-in options to view, print, and save downloaded GIF and JPEG images. It also has a built-in sound player, and provision for the use of helper applications. It has better security features than NCSA *Mosaic*, including facilities for payments over the Web.

One of the minor disadvantages of this product, is that when you retrieve a document, Spyglass *Enhanced Mosaic* shows the URL at the bottom of the screen, but provides no information about the size of the file, or progress with downloading.

Spyglass *Mosaic* has been incorporated into other Internet products by a variety of software producers. The most notable derivations of Spyglass *Mosaic* are Microsoft *Internet Explorer*, and IBM *Internet Connection for Windows*, a package of Internet tools that includes IBM *WebExplorer*.

Spyglass *Mosaic* is also found in *Internet in a Box*, a product from the CompuServe BBS which is designed to enable their *Windows* clients to access the Internet. It is also included in *Mosaic in a Box*, a package specially designed for accessing the Web through CompuServe, and *Internet Office*, a package for enabling *Windows* LANs and WANs to use the Internet via CompuServe.

IBM WebExplorer

IBM *Internet Connection for Windows* is a package of Internet tools, which provides for easy and seamless connection to IBM's

Internet access service, known as the IBM Global Network (or 'Advantis'). The package includes *WebExplorer*, a browser originally developed from Spyglass Mosaic. *WebExplorer* has been specially tailored for the IBM *OS/2 Warp* operating system. It will not work with Microsoft *Windows*, and neither is there a Macintosh version. Since it comes as standard with every new *OS/2 Warp* system, *WebExplorer* is guaranteed to become widely used, irrespective of its merits as a browser. The browser can also be used with dial-up Internet vendors other than IBM, and from within LANs connected to the Internet.

Perhaps one of the biggest advantages of this browser for *OS/2 Warp* users is that it has been customised to work within the *OS/2 Warp* environment, which makes it easy to access and very stable during use. Since it comes as standard with new versions of *OS/2 Warp*, installation problems are avoided, although it can be installed on older versions of *OS/2*.

WebExplorer is fairly full-featured, including buttons and pull-down menus, and a hotlist. It is particularly quick and easy to configure your set-up preferences, such as display fonts and colours. It also supports third-party helper applications. *WebExplorer* has a number of interesting features. *WebExplorer* allows you to have more than one Web page open at once, and you can also have more than one session of *WebExplorer* running simultaneously. Most browsers provide 'back' and buttons to enable the user to retrieve recently viewed Web pages, but a novel feature of *WebExplorer* is that this method is replaced by a visual map of your exploration of the Web. This more sophisticated approach to navigating the Web works well.

Microsoft Internet Explorer
Microsoft *Internet Explorer* has been developed from Spyglass' *Mosaic* browser, specifically for Microsoft *Windows*. The latest version of *Internet Explorer* is the official browser for the *Windows 95* operating system, and the Microsoft Network.

Security is a strong point of *Internet Explorer*. Like many other browsers, it supports Secure Sockets Layer (SSL) technology and RSA encryption. In addition, *Internet Explorer* supports Private Communication Technology (PCT), an upgrade to the SSL protocol, and Secure Transaction Technology (STT), an electronic payment technology developed by Microsoft and Visa International.

The browser supports many new developments in HTML extensions, such as HTML v. 3.0 tables, and more advanced Web page features, such as in-line embedded videos, scrolling banners, background audio and context-sensitive menus. The latest version of *Internet Explorer* is fully integrated with *Windows 95*. It includes an Internet tutorial and comprehensive search engine, supports full drag and drop of text and graphics. The *Internet Explorer* package also includes the RealAudio player (see Chapter 2), and provides access to Network News. The browser is currently freeware.

MacWeb and winWeb

MacWeb and *winWeb* are produced by Tradewave and are both freeware. The MacWeb was initially developed at the Microelectronics and Computer Technology Corporation (MCC) a consortium of major US high-technology firms, by the Enterprise Integration Network Group. This became EINet Corporation, and more recently, Tradewave.

MacWeb and *winWeb* provide similar window and mouse driven access to the Web, on Macintoshes and PCs running *Windows*, respectively. These packages provide most of the basic browser facilities, including: a hotlist (bookmark) facility, a history list, multiple Web windows, FTP and Gopher support, in-line GIF images, support for helper applications, and facilities for making secure Internet links. Preferences for fonts, colours, and the home page are easily changed. There is an innovative bookmark feature for treating URLs like files, making saving, organising, and retrieving them very fast. There is also a built-in newsreader facility for Network News. E-mail may also be sent using the mailto: URL. Other features include downloading text before graphics, and downloading status reporting.

MacWeb and *winWeb* had a reputation for being relatively more prone to crashing than products such as *Netscape*, but the latest versions are much more stable than their predecessors.

Commercial versions of Tradewave's browsers are due out soon, which will be much enhanced, providing features such as background images, in-line JPEG display, and support for many extended HTML features.

Cello

Cello is produced by Thomas Bruce at the Cornell Law School

Legal Information Institute, and is available for users of *Windows*. It is a freeware program, and provides basic browser facilities, but does not have the extra facilities of the commercial browsers, or semi-commercial programs like *Netscape*. It is perhaps most comparable in performance to other freeware programs such as NCSA *Mosaic*.

This said, it does allow you to follow hypertext links to newsgroups, and to send e-mail, which not all packages can do. It can also handle Telnet, FTP and WAIS connections. Its facilities for handling in-line images are rather crude however, leading to poor quality displays. Also, text spacing is commonly not what it should be. There is currently no support for forms, and no button bar, although these features are promised in the forthcoming versions of *Cello*.

Chapter 9

CREATING WEB PAGES

Why Create Your Own Web Pages?
Most users of the Web spend their time reading and looking at Web pages, and occasionally downloading items of interest onto their computers. However, anyone who has a direct and (preferably) permanent connection to the Internet can also create their own Web pages on their PC or Macintosh, and allow other users of the Internet to access them. By doing so, you are creating your own Web server, and you will need special Web server software, as described below. You will also need special software to help you to create the actual Web pages.

Creating your own Web server is a way of making information that you have available to the whole Internet community. Such information can be anything you like, such as: articles or papers you or friends have written, or even full novels; information about your business; your business' product catalogue; services you provide; your CV for potential employers to peruse; artwork or music you have produced; photos or video clips you have taken; a guide to your favourite Web pages; or a guide to your local area. For businesses, the Web provides an easy and economical means to advertise to a large (30 million plus) worldwide audience, which is thought to be relatively well educated and affluent. For academics, the Web provides a means of making data, results, and papers more widely available, increasing communication and understanding of research problems.

The hypermedia nature of the Web means that almost any type of material can be included. Neither is their any limit to the amount of information you can include, provided you have enough disc storage space on your computer.

What You Need
If you are going to provide a Web server on the Internet, you must be prepared to let other users of the Internet access the Web pages that you create. You will require special Web server

software running continuously on your computer, which allows Internet users to retrieve the Web pages you have set up, without allowing them to access your personal files or do any damage to your computer. Your computer, Web server software and network connections should be left running 24 hours a day, otherwise people will get blank screens and error messages if they try and access your Web pages when your computer is not connected. Remember that people living in other parts of the World will be in different time zones, and may well want to access your Web pages in the middle of your night, or at other odd hours of the day.

Web server software uses HTTP (Hypertext Transfer Protocol), and there are several HTTP applications to choose from. If you want to continue using your computer for other purposes, besides being a Web server, you may also want to limit the number of accesses, or 'hits' on your computer, so that your computer does not spend all its time answering requests for Web pages, and thus becoming slow and unresponsive.

Furthermore, you must have your own unique Internet address, so your computer must be directly connected to the Internet, e.g. via a LAN connected to the Internet, or via a dial-in SL/IP or PPP connection. Indirect connections, as typically provided by BBSs, are not adequate.

You must have permission from your Internet provider before you set up your computer as a Web server, since they will have to bear the impact of Internet users around the world accessing your computer via their Internet connections. Setting up your computer as a Web server will undoubtedly use their resources, which may be limited and unable to sustain large amounts of Internet traffic. They may therefore not be pleased, if you do not first seek and obtain permission.

To create your own Web pages you must learn the basics of HTML (Hypertext Mark-up Language). This is the simple code, or computer language, that is used to create the layout and of your Web pages, and provide links to other files. The code is downloaded by browser programs and used to create Web pages for display. There are special programs available which help you to create HTML documents, both for PCs and Macintoshes, so learning this language is not as hard a task as it might seem.

Hypertext Mark-up Language

The HTML language is officially under the control of an IETF (Internet Engineering Task Force) Working Group. At the time of writing the latest officially released version of HTML is version 2.0. However, the version 3.0 standard has almost been completed. Netscape Communications, producers of the popular browser *Netscape*, have released their own extensions to HTML which do not conform to HTML 3.0. They are under some pressure to conform, but *Netscape*'s market dominance may mean that their extensions are eventually adopted as standard by most producers of Web software, rather than HTML 3.0.

HTML documents are simple text-only documents that include codes which dictate how the document should be displayed by the Web browser, once downloaded. If you want to see what the HTML code looks like, some Web browser programs allow you to see the HTML code for any Web page you select. For example, *Netscape* users need only select the 'Source' option, and the HTML source code for the current Web page will be displayed.

Some typical HTML code looks like this:

```
<HTML>
<HEAD>
<TITLE>The World Wide Web Initiative: The
Project</TITLE>
</HEAD>
<BODY>

<H1> <IMG alt="WWW"
SRC="/hypertext/WWW/Icons/WWW/WWWlogo.gif">
The World Wide Web</H1>

<hr>
<H2><img alt="W3C"
src="/hypertext/WWW/Icons/WWW/w3c_96x67" alt="The
World Wide Web Consortium"></H2>

The <a href="/hypertext/WWW/Consortium/">World Wide
Web Consortium</a> promotes the Web by producing <a
href="#zSpecifications">specifications</a> and <a
href="#zReference">reference software</a>. W3C is funded
```

by industrial members but its products are freely available to all.

As can be seen in this example, the coding is not unduly complex. The mark-up codes are always enclosed within '<' and '>' characters. Text not enclosed within these characters will be displayed directly on the screen when the Web page is displayed. Mark-up codes enclosed by '<' and '>' are often called 'tags'. Usually, there are beginning and ending tags, with a slash '/' in front of the text in the ending tag. In the above example, the first two tags are *<HTML>* and *<HEAD>*, which do not require beginnings and endings, but *<TITLE>* and *</TITLE>* define the beginning and ending respectively.

In this short example, the document starts by defining that the rest of the document is written in HTML. This is followed by the title of the Web page, which is used for identification of the page within the Web. The first thing that actually gets displayed on screen when the Web page is accessed, is either a heading 'WWW', or, if your browser is set to display images, a GIF image called *logo.gif*. The *alt* code is short for 'alternative', and the *img* code is short for 'image'. The HTML codes tell us that the image is located in a directory on the Web server's hard disc called */hypertext/WWW/Icons/WWW.* This is in turn followed by the first (top) level heading 'The World Wide Web'. After this comes a horizontal break as indicated by the code *<hr>*, and then, either the heading 'W3C' and 'The World Wide Web Consortium', or the image called *w3c_96x67*. This ends the second level heading. There follows a paragraph of text, within which there are three hypertext links, indicated by the code *href*. The first *href* points gives the directory path to the required document. The following two *href* codes point to particular portions of the same Web page, as indicated by the use of the # character.

Although not shown in the example above, the *href code* can also be used to provide the user with a hypertext link to a resource on another Internet computer. For example:

<a href="http://home.netscape.com/index.html">Netscape Index</a>

When interpreted by a browser, this line of HTML would cause 'Netscape Index' to be displayed as a hypertext link on the

screen. When the link is selected by the user, it would cause the browser to connect to the Internet computer with the host name *home.netscape.com* and download a Web page with the file name *index.html*.

In this book we do not have the space to give a full description of HTML, but as you can see, it is quite easy to pick up. There are many detailed guides to HTML and authoring Web pages which are available via the Web, e.g.:

http://home.mcom.com/home/how-to-create-web-services.html
http://www.pcweek.ziff.com/~eamonn/crash_course.html
http://scholar.lib.vt.edu/reports/soasis-slides/HTML-Intro.html
http://fire.clarkson.edu/doc/html/htut.html

If you understand the principles of HTML, it can be written using any ordinary text editor program or wordprocessor. To help you write HTML on a wordprocessor, there are also special 'templates' which can be used, as described below. Another option is to use a special program dedicated to producing HTML documents. Such programs insulate the user from the details of the language, and Web pages may be created without knowing much about HTML.

Web Page Creation Software
There are quite a variety of HTML editor programs available for PCs and Macintoshes, many of which are freeware and shareware. Some editors are WYSIWYG (What You See Is What You Get), whilst others help you write HTML by allowing you to select the HTML codes from a menu and insert them at the relevant points.

Arguably one of the most popular *Windows* programs for creating HTML documents is SoftQuad *HoTMetaL*, which is a relatively easy to use WYSIWYG editor. *HoTMetaL* is context-sensitive, which helps in creation of new HTML documents and in editing old ones. A commercial version is available for purchase from SoftQuad called *HoTMetaL Pro*, which has a greater selection of functions, but does require quite a large amount of memory to run.

Live Markup and *Live Markup Pro*, both produced by MediaTech, are WYSIWYG HTML editors for Windows which insulate the user completely from HTML itself.

Also for *Windows* users, there is a non-WYSIWYG editor called *HTML Assistant*, from Brooklyn North Software Works. There is also a commercial version, *HTML Assistant Pro*, available from the same software publishers. This program is essentially a text editor with extra buttons which allow insertion of HTML tags, but there are a variety of features which help in the creation of HTML documents, including a preview option allowing you to see the finished Web page, and a good help facility.

A newer *Windows* HTML editor, which is also non-WYSIWYG, is the *HotDog Web Editor* from Sausage Software. The software is shareware and is available from the company's Web sites. The editor has gained in popularity quickly, since it offers a number of useful features. Most importantly, it supports both *Netscape* and the new HTML version 3.0 extensions to HTML. Dialogue boxes make creating forms and tables simple. The user can insert links, images, and text files by dragging them from File Manager or the internal *HotDog* file manager.

WebEdit is another *Windows* HTML editor which is mostly compliant with HTML version 3.0. *WebEdit* is shareware, produced by Nesbitt Software and published by KnowledgeWorks, Inc. The program provides for in-line figures, mathematical formulae, tabs, and banners. It includes a WYSIWYG table builder: simply enter your data into a spreadsheet-style grid, and *WebEdit* writes the HTML code. The user can define their own tags, and standard tags may be selected from toolbars. Also, the user can drag-and-drop in-line images and hypertext links into Web documents. The program also provides a spelling check facility.

Another simple, useful non-WYSIWYG HTML editor that is compatible with most Web browsers is *HTML Writer*. This editor is freeware, written by Kris Nosack at Brigham Young University, Utah. *HTMLed* and the commercial version *HTMLed Pro,* from Internet Software Technologies, are full-featured *Windows* editors for HTML. *HTMLed Pro* is fully *Netscape* compatible.

WEB Wizard, also known as the *Duke of URL*, is another commercial HTML package from the ARTA Software Group. This program provides a simple but quick way of generating Web pages. *WEB Wizard* interviews you about what you would like on your Web pages, and then outputs a HTML file. The results are not very fancy, but the program is easy to use.

There are also 'wordprocessor templates' designed to work in conjunction with wordprocessor programs. For *Windows* users, Microsoft has released *Internet Assistant*, a *Word for Windows* template which enables editing of HTML in a WYSIWYG manner, and provides the ability to load existing HTML documents. It also includes some browsing capabilities, sufficient to assist in editing.

ANT_HTML is another Microsoft *Word* template for both *Windows* and Macintoshes, available from the EINet FTP archive, which can convert Microsoft Word documents into HTML documents in a WYSIWYG environment. Although it is useful for creating HTML documents, it cannot be used for editing existing HTML documents. For this, use the *ANT_PLUS* utility program, which converts existing HTML files for importation and further editing in Microsoft *Word*.

For fans of the Novell *WordPerfect* wordprocessor package, there is *WordPerfect to HTML*, which is a set of templates that allow WordPerfect documents to be prepared for HTML. It is notable that most *Windows* HTML editors leave out table-making capabilities. Jordan Evans' *Excel 5.0 to HTML Table Converter* is one program that provides this facility. It can convert Microsoft Excel spreadsheets into HTML format.

A comprehensive list of HTML editors for *Windows* and DOS systems is kept at the 'Yahoo' Web site:

http://www.yahoo.com/Computers_and_Internet/Internet/World_Wide_Web/HTML_Editors/MS_Windows/
http://www.yahoo.com/Computers_and_Internet/Internet/World_Wide_Web/HTML_Editors/DOS/

There are also dedicated HTML creation programs for Macintoshes. For example, there is *Simple HTML Editor*, which requires the Apple *HyperCard* program. This is freeware and available by FTP from Macintosh software archives. *Simple HTML Editor* makes creating HTML documents relatively simple, although it is not so suitable for large HTML documents.

Also for Macintosh users, *BBEdit* is a powerful text editor that provides a mechanism so that you can develop your own external commands, such as HTML extensions. *BBEdit* is a commercial product from Bare Bones Software. There is a demo version and a freeware, less complete version called *BBEdit Lite*,

available via anonymous FTP from Macintosh Internet archives. The *BBEdit HTML Extensions* are also freeware, and work with both versions of *BBEdit*.

HTML.edit is a popular HTML writing utility for Macintoshes, available by FTP from most archives. This program is written using Apple *Hypercard* but does not require a *HyperCard* program in order to run. HTML tags are easily inserted into text using this program, and there are a number of useful editing features. The way that the program uses Hypercard can be confusing though.

HTML Editor is a good value shareware Macintosh program for producing HTML, being relatively easy to use and bug-free. Again, it is available from a variety of anonymous FTP sites. It is a non-WYSIWYG editor, but does give you a preview option, so you may see what your Web page looks like. It has a large selection of available tags, or you can define your own, and it can handle large files and non-standard HTML files reasonably well.

Other Macintosh HTML editors include *HTML Grinder, HTML Pro, HTML SuperText, HTML Writer, Webtor*, and *HTML Web Weaver*. A current list of available HTML editors for Macintosh computers can be found on the 'Yahoo' Web site:

http://www.yahoo.com/Computers_and_Internet/Internet/World_Wide_Web/HTML_Editors/Macintosh/

In addition to using a HTML editor program to create Web pages, if you wish to include photographs and other graphics, you will need other specialist graphics software. Most people incorporate photos in their Web pages using either GIF or JPEG formats, and there are a large number of freeware and shareware programs around which handle these formats.

Popular programs for displaying and editing GIF and JPEG images include *WinGIF, LVIEW*, and *JPEGView* for *Windows* users, and *GIFConverter* for Macintosh users. A popular commercial package for image handling on a Macintosh is Adobe *Photoshop*. Similarly, if you wish to include audio and video clips in your Web pages, you will need to use appropriate software for manipulating audio and video files.

Web Server Software
Web server software provides a link between data held on a Web

server computer and the client computers which request that data, and occasionally send data in return. Data is moved around the Web using the system known as HTTP (Hypertext Transfer Protocol). Web server programs use HTTP to communicate with Web browser programs on client computers. HTTP relies on TCP/IP being available in order to transmit the stream of binary data. For modem users this will mean having a PPP, SL/IP or ARA connection. Given that, then an HTTP data transfer consists of four operations. Firstly, the Web browser program, which resides on a client computer, opens a TCP/IP connection to a Web server computer on the Internet. Secondly, a request for data is sent to the server. Thirdly, the server sends the requested data back to the browser. Lastly, the browser disconnects the client computer from the server computer. It is then the job of the browser to handle the data appropriately. Depending on the type of data, this may mean displaying it as a Web page, displaying it as a separate image, playing it as a sound, playing it as a video clip, or saving it as a file on disc.

Since the HTTP connection is opened only when data is required and closed immediately afterwards, Web programs are said to be 'stateless'. They can be contrasted with older methods of accessing the Internet, such as FTP, in which the connection to the remote computer is continuous and maintained whether or not data is actually being transferred. Connection methods which are not stateless, such as FTP, can more easily cause Internet servers to become overloaded, and greatly increase the traffic on the Internet. Therefore, HTTP is much kinder to the Internet, using its resources more efficiently.

HTTP Web server programs are available for basic *Windows*, *OS/2* and DOS systems, as well as PC LAN systems running Novell *Netware* and Microsoft *Windows NT*.

Netscape Communications Corporation offers two Web server products, neither of which are available free. The more powerful *Netscape Commerce Server* is capable of secure transactions, and is thus ideal if you wish to carry out financial transactions via the Web. There is also the cheaper *Netscape Communications Server*. Both are very efficient and better than many of the freeware and shareware server programs currently available.

Other PC Web server programs include *KA9Q NOS*, a shareware Internet server package for DOS that includes HTTP

capability. Another package, *Windows httpd*, is a *Windows* version of a Unix program which has proved popular. *SerWeb* is a simple, effective Web server for Windows written by Gustavo Estrella. *Goserve* is a Web server program for *OS/2*, and is particularly easy to install. *OS2HTTPD* is another Web server for *OS/2* and *Windows NT*, written by Frankie Fan. *Chameleon Web Personal Server* is a server program which comes with *Chameleon* TCP/IP software from NetManage. The shareware program *HTTPS* provides a good Web server for those running Microsoft *Windows NT*. A professional version of *HTTPS* is also available. *Purveyor* from Process Software Corporation is another *Windows NT* Web server program. *GLACI-HTTPD*, from The Great Lakes Area Commercial Internet, is a software module which allows a Novell *NetWare* LAN server to become a Web server also.

A current list of popular HTTP server programs for PCs (and other computers) is kept at the 'Yahoo' site:

http://www.yahoo.com/Computers_and_Internet/Internet/World_Wide_Web/HTTP/Servers/

A popular shareware Web server program for Macintoshes is *MacHTTP*, which provides a full system for administering your own Web server. There is now a commercial version available from StarNine Technologies, called *WebSTAR*, which has extra facilities, and is *Netscape* compatible. A list of Macintosh HTTP servers is maintained at the 'Yahoo' site:

http://www.yahoo.com/Computers_and_Internet/Internet/World_Wide_Web/HTTP/Servers/Macintosh/

HTTP only requires a network which uses TCP/IP, so can be used on most LANs, not just the Internet. So, this means that any institution which has a TCP/IP LAN can set up an internal Web system, irrespective of whether they are connected to the Internet. Any of the HTTP server packages described above can be used to set up a Web server within the LAN, which ideally would be a high-performance PC or Macintosh. Other computers on the network can then access Web pages and other data on the server, using one of the Web browser programs described in this book.

Appendix 1

GLOSSARY

Anchor A term used to describe a HTML command that defines a hypertext link, and the link itself.

Anonymous FTP Anonymous File Transfer Protocol. A standard method which allows a person at one computer to log-in to another computer with the username 'anonymous' and transfer files between the computers. Note that the person does not need to be registered on the remote computer, but the remote computer does need to be specially configured to accept anonymous FTP. FTP programs are abundant for PCs, Macintoshes and many other types of computer.

Apple Computers A US-based multinational company which makes the Macintosh, Quadra and Power Macintosh, and a whole host of printers, scanners, and other peripherals. Apple Computers were amongst the first to popularise the use of windows and icons as a method of controlling desktop computers. Apple Computers do not make PCs, which have for many years rivalled Apple's range of computers.

Application This is another term for a computer program, or suite of programs. The term is usually used to describe a utility program with which the user has direct interaction, such as a word-processing program, or a spreadsheet program, rather than a program with which the interaction is not so direct, such as an operating system program. The term is also generally not used to describe game programs.

Archie A program found on many Internet host computers, which allows the user to conduct searches for particular files across the Internet. Archie will list file and directory locations comprising host computer names and directory paths.

ARPANET Advanced Research Projects Agency Network. The forerunner of the modern Internet which was established in 1969 for the United States military, and eventually dismantled in 1990.

ASCII American Standard Code for Information Interchange. ASCII provides a way of representing ordinary alphabetic, numeric and keyboard characters as binary numbers, using 128 ASCII codes. An ASCII character file is a very common, simple way of storing text in a computer or on a disc. ASCII can also be used to code and store any kind of binary file.

Authoring The process of producing a Web hypertext document.

Backbone A network which provides a vital connection between other networks, and without which the other networks cannot communicate. Backbone networks which support the Internet include the NSFNET in the USA, and JANET in the UK.

Back-link A hypertext link which returns you to a previously viewed hypertext document.

Bandwidth The bandwith of a communications channel is the highest frequency with which data is transmitted. The bandwidth of a transmission is the range of frequencies present in the signal. By coding signals digitally and transmitting them on different frequencies, many transmissions may be 'stacked' in a single channel and sent simultaneously without mutual interference. Signals vary in bandwidth depending on how fast data is transmitted. High-speed transmission of large data volumes requires high bandwidths.

Baud In a binary system, the Baud rate is the number of bits transmitted per second. This is one way of measuring the speed at which computer data is transmitted. This measure is now used much less frequently than the alternative bps (bits per second).

BBS Bulletin Board System. Originally this meant a computer network that provided users with the ability to contribute news and messages, and allowed all other users to read these contributions, and if they wished, respond to them. Most BBSs are now

commercial, and provide users with many other services, such as Internet access, electronic mail, news and weather information, etc.

Binary A counting system that uses ones and zeros only, rather than the decimal digits zero through to nine. All computers function at their most basic level by using binary, since they run on electricity, and electricity can be used to code one (on) and zero (off).

BinHex A method for coding any computer file using ASCII characters only (i.e. text). Also the name of a program that can code and decode BinHex files.

Bit Binary digit, i.e. one or zero. Bits are a useful way of expressing the two main electrical states, respectively on and off. Any number that can be expressed using the binary counting system can be represented using a series of bits.

Bit-map A method for storing pictures or letters on a screen or in a file using binary code.

BITNET Because It's There Network, or alternatively, Because It's Time Network. A co-operative network for academic institutions established in the USA, but now used around the world. It is more primitive than the Internet, being best for electronic mail and file transfer only, rather than interactive services such as Telnet.

Bookmarks A Web browser user may choose to keep the URLs of favourite Web pages, or other resources, on a special list, known as a 'bookmark list' or 'hotlist'. Most Web browsers provide this facility. Bookmarks may then be selected by the user at any later date, in order to quickly retrieve the corresponding Web resource. Bookmarks only need to be updated when a URL is changed.

bps Bits per second. This specifies the speed of data transfer, defined by the number of bits (binary digits) transferred per second. The term is often used to describe the speed at which networks and modems work.

Browser A program used to explore the Web. The program provides a means of viewing Web pages and a way of moving from one to another. A browser is synonymous with a 'Web client' program, and a 'navigator' program.

Bug A fault within a program that causes the program to behave incorrectly, or even causes the program to stop working altogether, i.e. to 'crash'. Bugs are the responsibility of those who write the programs.

Bulletin board See BBS.

Button A symbol represented on-screen to look like a push-button, common to windows-based software, such as Macintosh, *OS/2* and Microsoft *Windows*, which can be selected by pointing with the mouse and pressing the mouse button. When the button is pushed, it tells the computer to carry out some particular instruction. Web pages often contain buttons, which act like other hypertext links. See link.

Byte A number consisting of 8 binary digits or 'bits'. In the decimal counting system, a byte can have values of 0–255. Data on a computer or hard disc is commonly stored as bytes, since a byte can represent one of up to 256 alphabetic, numeric and other characters.

Cache Pronounced 'cash', this term refers to the portion of memory or hard disc space on your computer, or on a proxy computer, which is reserved for storing temporary data, such as the most recently downloaded Web pages.

Card Another term for a short hypertext node or page, as used in Apple Computers *Hypercard* software.

Case sensitive Sometimes it does not make any difference whether you use upper case (capital) letters or lower case letters when entering text into a computer. If it is important that you use the correct case, then the computer or program is said to be 'case sensitive'.

CERN European Centre for Particle Physics, where the Web was first developed. The acronym stands for the original French name for the institution: "Conseil Europeen pour la Recherche Nucleaire".

CD-ROM Compact Disc-Read Only Memory. A disc upon which digital data has been pre-recorded, which can be read using a CD-ROM 'drive' connected to a computer. CD-ROM data is stored using optical techniques rather than the magnetic techniques that are used for conventional floppy discs, and hence data cannot be erased with magnetic fields. In fact, data on a CD-ROM may not be changed in any way. The technology is the same as that used for ordinary music CDs, hence CD-ROM drives can be used to play music CDs, providing your computer has a sound card, loudspeakers or headphone jack and the appropriate software.

Checkbox A graphics symbol which looks like a small square, which may or may not be filled with a cross, depending on whether the user has 'checked' it by pointing with the mouse and clicking the mouse button. A box which has been checked indicates that option has been selected. A checkbox works much like an on-off switch to select-deselect options. Checkboxes are used in many software packages and Web pages for users to select options.

CIX Compulink Information Exchange. A commercial network which uses the TCP/IP standard, and provides some BBS services.

Clickable maps See 'image maps'.

Client computer A computer which relies upon the resources of another, usually more powerful computer, to which it is connected. In a typical server-based network, all the computers connected to the server computer may be called clients.

Client program A program that relies upon the resources of another program, usually residing on another computer, to which there is a network connection. For example, a Web browser program on a PC or Macintosh is a type of client program, which

is used to access Web pages stored on another computer connected to the network.

Clipboard Users of *Windows* and Macintoshes always have a temporary file available for storing text and graphics, which is called the 'clipboard'. When you 'copy' or 'cut' text or graphics in a word processing package, graphics program, or any other application, the text or graphics is stored in the clipboard file. You can view what is in this file at any time by selecting the clipboard icon. When you use any application's 'paste' function, the contents of the clipboard are added to the file that you are working on with that application.

CompuServe One of the largest multinational Bulletin Board Systems and providers of Internet services to business and non-business clients.

Conference Part of a Bulletin Board System which is set aside for discussion and messaging on a chosen subject.

CPU Central Processing Unit. This is the silicon chip at the heart of every computer which performs all the logical operations, including calculations, under the direction of programs stored in the memory. CPUs are manufactured by a variety of manufacturers, and many different designs are available, with differing performance characteristics.

Crash When a program unexpectedly stops running, it is said to have 'crashed'. Sometimes this can also cause the computer on which the program is running to stop working, in which case the computer is said to have crashed. A crash usually necessitates that the program is re-started, and maybe the computer also. Crashes are commonly caused by program 'bugs', or by programs running simultaneously which conflict with each other. Loss of a network connection during a Web session may also cause a crash.

Cyberspace A buzz-word of the mid-1990's, meant to describe the world of human interaction which is taking place wholly via electronic means on the Internet.

Daemon A program which starts automatically and runs independently of the main program that is running on a networked computer. Daemons may perform various management tasks necessary to the proper functioning of the main program. The user often does not need to know that a daemon has been started, or when it has finished. On computers running the Unix operating system, 'daemon' often means 'server', because servers normally run independently.

Data Any type of information that may be stored or processed by a computer. Data is stored in files, usually in either ASCII or binary format.

Database A collection of information or data, which is arranged in an orderly manner and stored in some kind of system which allows the data to be retrieved. There are large computer databases all over the world, many of which can be reached via the Internet. The Internet itself may be viewed as a large database distributed across a network.

Device Any piece of hardware other than a computer, such as a printer, a plotter, a scanner or a CD-ROM.

Dialogue box An on-screen box found in Macintosh windows or Microsoft Windows, in which you can make choices about what you want the computer to do next.

Directory This is a collection of files which have all been stored under a common name, on a hard disc or diskette. There are various ways of referring to a directory. In DOS, Unix, and VMS, directories have long names, depending on which disc drive they are on, and if they are themselves contained within another directory. In windows operating systems, such as that used on Macintoshes and Microsoft *Windows,* the directories are represented by icons. These icons often look like folders, and are referred to as such.

Disc cache See 'cache'.

Disc drive An electronic device which will read and write magnetically coded data to and from a diskette or a hard disc. All

PCs and Macintoshes have at least two disc drives, one for diskettes and one for the hard disc inside the computer.

Diskette See 'floppy disc'.

DNS Domain Name System. A hierarchical system for naming computers connected to the Internet, based on their country, their institutional affiliation, and local computer name. The DNS is used for IP host names.

Domain Part of an IP host name.

Domain Name Server A computer that is connected to a network and has been set up so that it is able to supply domain names and IP addresses of other computers that are linked to it.

DOS Disc Operating System. This is a simple computer language which allows the user to control computer disc drives and other basic functions. IBM, Microsoft, and Novell all produce DOS programs for PCs. The PC is controlled by typing simple text commands. Microsoft *Windows 95* is more complex, since it is a DOS system and a windows system combined. Similarly, *System 7* from Apple Computers allows full control of a Macintosh and its disc system using icons and windows. Note that when most people refer to DOS, they are referring to the DOS on a PC, but strictly speaking, every computer has a DOS installed.

Download This is the process of moving or copying a file (i.e. data or program) from a larger computer onto a smaller computer. When you are connected to a large network, or bulletin board, you will commonly be downloading files onto your PC or Macintosh.

Ecash Electronic cash. This is a method for making cash payments via the Internet, popularised by the DigiCash company.

E-mail Electronic mail. A message or computer file with a standard header, which is sent from one networked user to another. The other user may be on your LAN, or may be on the other side of the world.

E-text Electronic text. A book, poem, play or other work of litera-ture, which has been stored in digital form. E-texts are commonly non-copyrighted works, available to the general public via the Web.

Encryption A method for making a password secret. The pass-word is coded in such a way that it cannot easily be read.

Ethernet An international standard LAN technology, comprising specialised cables, adapter cards and associated software. This is probably the most popular and widespread LAN technology. Originally developed by Xerox, Ethernet was later standardised by Xerox, Digital Equipment and Intel. This is known as IEEE (Institution of Electrical and Electronic Engineers) standard 802.3. Three types of Ethernet cable now exist: Thin, Thick and Twisted-Pair.

E-zine Electronic magazine. A magazine published on the Web, rather than as a conventional printed publication.

FAQ Frequently Asked Questions. This is a document, common-ly posted to a Network News group, which attempts to answer network users' most commonly asked questions. If you join a new newsgroup, try to read the FAQ, before asking the other readers too many questions about the newsgroup. FAQs are now also commonly available as Web pages.

File This is a block of data (text or other information), or a program, which is a discrete entity and has its own name. A file can be recorded on a hard disc drive or a diskette, sent to a peripheral device such as printer, or sent across a network.

File extension Refers to the part of a file name after the full-stop, e.g. *readme.txt* has the file extension txt. The file extension is usually only three letters and indicates the type of file and/or how it was produced, e.g. *txt* indicates that the file contains text. File extensions will be familiar to PC users but are rarely used for Macintosh files, since Macintosh files nearly always have an associated icon, which provides a visual description of the file type and usually also the program which produced it.

Firewall A method for protecting certain portions of a computer hard disc, or parts of a private computer network, from intrusion by unauthorised users. Many companies that provide access to the Internet for their employees use a firewall to prevent outsiders from gaining unauthorised access to company computers via the Internet.

Floppy disc Also known as a diskette. This is a circular piece of magnetic material, which is indeed floppy, but is housed inside a rigid protective covering. Two main sizes exist. Diskettes that are 3.5 inches across are now most common, and are protected by a rigid plastic shell. 5.25 inch diskettes are now rare, but still available, and these are protected by a much thinner, flexible shell. The latter are more easily damaged. Most computers have a disc drive device that will record and retrieve programs and data from diskettes.

Font Describes a set of characters, which have the same size and style. The British spelling of the word is 'fount', but the American English spelling is now so popularised, that we use 'font' in this book. Examples of commonly used fonts are 'Times', which is used in many newspapers, and 'Courier', which is the font produced by old-fashioned typewriters. The size of a font is described in terms of points. Printed pages of text typically use fonts between 9 and 12 point in size. Two main types of font are used on Web pages: proportional and fixed. Most Web pages use a proportional font, whereby each character is only as wide as is necessary. Fixed fonts have characters each with a fixed width, and are thus called monospaced. Fixed font is used when the text layout must be precise. Fixed and proportional fonts may be chosen using your browser.

Form A Web page which allows the viewer to enter text into special boxes. The information entered is then sent back to the authors of the Web page.

Freeware Software that is available for anyone to use, and does not need to be paid for. There is a plentiful supply of freeware available over the Internet. Not to be confused with shareware.

FTP File Transfer Protocol. A standard method which allows a person at one computer to log-in to another computer and transfer files between the computers. Programs that utilise FTP are abundant for PCs, Macintoshes and many other types of computer.

Gateway A computer link which allows two or more networks to communicate. All information and data which is sent from one network to another must go via the gateway. E-mail gateways are one example, allowing e-mail to be sent from one type of network to another.

Gb Gigabyte. One thousand million bytes. One byte is the equivalent of one alphabetic or numeric character. This term is generally used to define the size of computer memories and discs.

GIF Graphics Interchange Format. A binary data format for storing pictures.

Gigabyte See 'Gb'

Gopher A method for browsing the Internet and information stored in various large computers around the World. Users control Gopher via menus and simple commands. Files can also be downloaded using Gopher.

GUI Graphical User Interface. This is a way of controlling your computer by activating pictures (icons) which represent applications and files. Macintosh *System 7* is a GUI, and so is Microsoft *Windows*.

Hacker Originally this term was meant to describe someone who uses a computer with great skill and aptitude, and it was not meant to be a derogatory term at all. Now it is reserved for those who make unauthorised entries into computer networks, and who set about destroying files, copying files, and generally creating mayhem.

Hard disc Also referred to as 'hard disc drive' or 'hard drive'. This comprises a stack of magnetically coated aluminium discs

fixed onto a spindle, which is housed inside your computer, and upon which programs and data can be stored. External hard disks sit outside the main computer housing, in a separate case.

Hardware This means the actual computer, printer, disc drive etc., comprising silicon chips, plastic and metal. It specifically does not include the actual computer programs, called 'software', which are used to operate the hardware.

Header Information given at the top of a document or file, usually detailing what the document or file is about. For example, a word-processor text document may have a header that is printed at the top of each page and gives the title of the document. A computer file normally has a header that describes the file type, how the code is set out, how large the file is, etc. An e-mail message also has a header that describes who it is from, who it is to, when it was sent, etc.

Helper A program used in conjunction with a Web browser program. The Web browser program calls upon the helper program in order to carry out tasks it cannot perform itself, such as displaying an image, playing an audio file, etc.

Hit The term used to describe one access, or retrieval of a Web page, by an Internet user. Those who provide Web pages can record how many 'hits' they get on their pages, and for a popular page, there may be many thousands of 'hits' per day.

Home directory The part of a hard disc on a LAN server computer or multi-user computer where users keep their personal files.

Homepage A special kind of Web page designed to welcome visitors to a Web server, provide information about that server, and links to other Web documents on that server. Also, the term is used to describe the first Web page (if any) loaded automatically when a browser is started .

Host computer A computer on a network which allows remote users to use its facilities, i.e. it acts as a host. For example, most Internet computers are host computers. See 'IP host name' and

'IP host number'. Also synonymous with 'node', but see definition of node for an alternative meaning.

Host name See 'IP host name'.

Hotlist Another name for a bookmark list. See 'bookmarks'.

HTML Hypertext Mark-up Language. The computer language which is used to produce hypertext documents for the Web, i.e. Web pages. The language comprises simple text codes which describe text formats and layout, links to other Web pages, and links to hypermedia resources such as images. There are currently several versions of HTML in use worldwide. Version 2.0 is in widespread use, but is rapidly being superseded by version 3.0. There are extensions (additions) to both standards, which are specific to certain browsers. The most popular are those used by the *Netscape* browser.

HTTP Hypertext Transfer Protocol. A public domain communication language for computer networks, compatible with the TCP/IP standards, particularly useful for linking text databases on networked computers. Although it does not completely comply with the original HTTP standard, the Web uses a HTTP-like system.

HTTPS Hypertext Transfer Protocol which uses SSL data security. Similar to normal HTTP, but with built-in facilities for secure data transfer, using the public-key encryption system RSA.

Hyperlink Short for 'hypertext link'. See 'link'.

Hypermedia An extension of 'hypertext', which includes images, sound and video, as well as text. The appearance of hyper-media is comparable to multimedia. See 'hypertext' and 'multimedia'.

Hypertext A method for linking pages of text within a computer database or network service by using highlighted 'link' words. By selecting link words, the user can move easily from reading one topic to another. The term is often used to mean 'hypermedia', although this is strictly incorrect.

IAB Internet Activities Board. An organisation responsible for steering and managing the development of the Internet.

IANA Internet Assigned Numbers Authority. An organisation in charge of assigning Internet Protocol code numbers.

IBM International Business Machines. A US-based multinational company which produced the original PC (Personal Computer), and is still producing its successors. However, many PCs are now made by companies other than IBM. IBM also produce a number of larger computers.

Icon A small picture which appears on a computer screen to represent a file, a program or some process that is taking place. It is used in conjunction with windows and a mouse to control the computer. Icons can be selected, moved, activated, and thrown away.

IETF Internet Engineering Task Force. A subsidiary of the IAB.

Image map Graphical components within a Web page which can link to more than one resource. The resource chosen depends on which part of the image the user selects with the computer mouse. Frequently, image maps are indeed actual geographical maps, but they need not be. They are also called 'clickable maps', since the user 'clicks' the mouse button when pointing to a particular part of the map.

Information Superhighway A buzzword of the mid-1990's, meant to describe the evolving interconnected electronic networks which are linking homes, offices, schools and universities around the World. The Internet represents the first crude incarnation of the Information Superhighway. Ultimately the Information Superhighway will develop into a very sophisticated, all-embracing world-wide network.

In-line A graphical item or image downloaded and displayed as part of a Web page, as opposed to one that needs to be downloaded and displayed separately from the Web page.

Input Data entered into a computer or program.

Installer A program designed to make installation of a software package onto a computer as easy as possible. An installer will automatically make allowances for the hardware and software already present. Although an installer may ask for some input from the user during the installation process, this should be minimal.

Internet A computer communications network started in the US in the 1970's, which has since grown to encompass more than 20 million users world wide. It now comprises a loosely connected collection of networks, which communicate using a collection of simple standard rules (protocols), known as TCP/IP. Although there is locally some regulation of the Internet, and there are volunteer groups responsible for guiding and steering the development of the Internet on a global scale, there is no absolute international control or ownership of the Internet. Internet software and hardware is sold by a variety of vendors in different countries. The most popular means of using the Internet is known as the World Wide Web.

IP Internet Protocol. These are the rules and standards of the Internet, which allow such a huge variety of computers and software packages to interact with the Internet, and with each other via the Internet.

IP host name Every computer connected to the Internet must have an identifying name, which is called the IP host name. The form is usually three to five alphabetic codes, separated by full-stops. These codes indicate the actual name of the computer or LAN, the organisation and type of organisation (academic, commercial, government or military), and the country.

IP host number Every computer connected to the Internet must have an identifying code number, which is called the IP number. The form of the IP host number is usually four numbers separated by full-stops.

IRC Internet Relay Chat. Invented by Jarkko Oikarinen of Finland in 1988, it is a multi-user chat system, where people convene on the Internet, using 'channels' to 'talk' privately or in groups. 'Talking' is achieved by entering text at the keyboard.

IRC is particularly popular amongst users of computers running the Unix operating system, but there are also programs which allow PC and Macintosh users to join in.

IRTF Internet Research Task Force. A subsidiary of the IAB.

ISOC The Internet Society. Founded in 1992 with the objective of overseeing the development of the Internet.

IT Information Technology. This is another term for the general field of computer communications and data/information retrieval.

JANET Joint Academic NETwork. An incarnation of the Internet which exists in the UK only. It was created jointly by British academic institutions.

JPEG A binary data format for storing pictures devised by the Joint Photographic Experts Group.

Jump Jargon used to describe the act of selecting a link on a Web page, leading to another resource. The term is misleading, since you do not actually 'jump' anywhere. Rather, selecting the link results in data being downloaded, i.e. brought to you.

Kb Kilobyte. One thousand bytes. One byte is the equivalent of one alphabetic or numeric character. This term is generally used to define the size of computer memories and discs.

Kermit An error-correcting file transfer protocol designed for connecting computers to a network with a dial-up link. It was developed at Columbia University in the early 1980's. It has been adapted for use with Ethernet networks.

Killer Application Also shortened to 'killer ap'. Meant to refer to the ultimate, or very best program for doing a particular task. For example, NCSA *Mosaic* was widely regarded as the killer application for the Web, until the rise in popularity of *Netscape*.

Kilobyte See Kb

Knowbot A contraction of 'knowledge robot'. A program designed to automatically search the Web for information, without the guidance of a human operator.

LAN Local Area Network. A group of computers which communicate with each other via special electrical cables, hardware and software. A LAN may also include printers, communal disc drives, and other peripherals. Typically, a LAN will encompass all the computers in one office, or in a few buildings at most.

Line browser A browser with no capability to display images of any kind.

Link A highlighted word, graphic symbol or picture embedded within a hypertext document, which when selected, causes another hypertext document to be retrieved and displayed, that is related to the chosen link.

Lite A term usually applied to a piece of software, for which there is also available a larger, more advanced version, which has more functions. The 'lite' version will usually be cheaper to buy than the other version, or even free. The other version is often called the 'pro' version, short for 'professional'.

LocalTalk A LAN system developed by the Apple Computer company for Macintoshes and Apple peripheral devices.

Log-in The process of entering a user name and password when beginning a session on a multi-user computer or network. Also known as 'log-on'.

Log-out The process of finishing a session on a multi-user computer or network. Also known as 'log-off'.

Machine A word commonly used instead of 'computer'.

Macintosh This name covers a whole family of computers produced by the Apple Computer company. Its functions and performance are broadly similar to PCs, although it has a different operating system and runs different software. The Macintosh uses a 'windows' based operating system, the current version of

which is called *System 7*, but this is not to be confused with the Microsoft *Windows* program for PCs.

Mailbox This is the location on a networked computer, that receives and stores a particular user's incoming e-mail messages. The mailbox always has a name, which is very often the same as the person's user name.

Mail folder A directory or folder on a disc that is used to store e-mail messages.

Mail program A computer program that handles e-mail.

MB Megabyte. One million bytes. One byte is the equivalent of one alphabetic or numeric character. This term is generally used to define the size of computer memories and disc.

Megabyte See MB.

Memory The silicon chips inside a computer that store data. See 'RAM' and 'ROM'.

Memory cache See 'cache'.

MIME Multipurpose Internet Mail Extensions. A method for encoding files, particularly useful for sending images, audio and video files via the Internet.

Mirror There are a large number of Internet software archives world wide. As well as their own software collections, many of these archives also keep copies of the software collections available at the other archives. These copies are known as mirrors. Mirrors are usually updated every few days or weeks. By using a local mirror of a distant archive, rather than connecting directly to the distant archive, you put less strain on the Internet, and you are more likely to get smooth, error-free downloading.

Modem An abbreviation for modulator/demodulator. This is a hardware device which may be installed inside your computer, or as a free-standing unit outside your computer. You must also have the appropriate software to run the modem, although this is

usually supplied with the modem. It allows you to connect your computer directly to a telephone line and thus enables you to send and receive data over the telephone.

Mouse The small gadget which sits beside most Macintoshes and PCs, with a lead connecting it to the computer, and one or more buttons on top. By sliding the mouse across the desk, preferably on a special mouse pad, and by pressing the mouse buttons, it is possible to control the computer, providing the computer is running software which recognises the mouse, as do all Macintoshes, and PCs running Microsoft *Windows*.

Multimedia Literally meaning many media, where the media are text, images, video and sound. Multimedia information is commonly stored on CD-ROMs, since the amount of code needed for multimedia is usually very large, and only CD-ROMs have a suitably high data storage capacity. The information can also be read more quickly from CD-ROMs than from most other devices, such as hard discs or diskettes. Much of the information available on the Web is also a form of multimedia, stored in a special format known as 'hypermedia', which also provides for links between documents that are actually embedded within the documents.

Multimedia computer A high performance Macintosh or PC which is better able to cope with multimedia by having a CD-ROM drive, large amounts of memory, a fast CPU and a high-resolution monitor.

Navigation The process of moving from one Web page to another, by following hypertext links.

Navigator A program that allows the user to retrieve and display pages from the Web, and to easily explore the Web. Such programs are more commonly called 'browsers'.

NCSA National Center for Supercomputing Applications. This institution in the USA has been responsible for the development of many network programs available freely to the public.

Net As in 'The Net', meaning the Internet.

Network A collection of computers and other devices such as printers and disk drives which are connected, such that they can communicate and send data from one to another.

Network News The world wide bulletin board system which is free to use, and is also known as 'Usenet' and 'Net News'.

Newsfeed A computer that provides users with the ability to read Network News.

Newsgroup A forum for discussion within Network News, which has a common theme.

Newsreader A program which allows the user to read Network News articles. A newsreader will also commonly provide a facility for replying to articles and submitting new articles.

NNTP Network News Transfer Protocol. A method of distributing Network News articles via a TCP/IP network such as the Internet.

Node A unit of hypertext which may be anything from a few words to many pages. Web pages and Apple Computers *Hypercard* cards are both examples of nodes. The term is also synonymous with a 'hypertext document'. In the context of computer network hardware, a node is also the name given to a network host computer.

NIC Network Information Center. An organisation responsible for assigning and distributing Internet addresses. Administered by SRI International of California.

NSFNET National Science Foundation Network. This network was started in the United States in 1986, and links major computing centres around the country.

Off-line Means having an inactive link to a computer network, particularly the Internet.

On-line Means having an active link to a computer network, particularly the Internet. The term is most commonly used as an adjective to describe any facility which is accessible via the

Internet, e.g. on-line library, on-line book, on-line help, on-line catalogue, on-line directory, etc.

OPAC On-line Public Access Catalogue. A computerised system for storing a library catalogue, used in many public and university libraries worldwide. Many OPACs are connected to the Internet, and may be accessed via Telnet, although Web access is becoming more common.

Operating system A program which controls the basic functions of a computer, such as the monitor screen, the keyboard and the disc drives.

OS/2 An operating system for PCs designed and produced by IBM. The latest version is called OS/2 Warp. Like Microsoft *Windows* and Apple *System 7*, this operating system provides user-friendly windows, pull-down menus and icons, which may be controlled using a mouse.

Outernet A network that is not a part of the Internet.

Output Results produced by a computer or program, which might be text, numbers, images, sound, or video.

Parallel port This is a socket at the back of a computer that receives or transmits data a byte at a time. It is sometimes called the 'printer port', since the socket can be used for connecting a printer. Compare with 'serial port'.

Password This is the secret code that a person on a multi-user computer network must enter when starting a session, i.e. logging-in. A password usually comprises about six alphanumeric characters.

Patch A piece of software or computer code that fixes software that does not work correctly.

Path This is a description of the route to a particular file, which may start with the name of the disc drive, followed by the name of a directory, followed by the names of any number of subdirectories, followed by the name of the file itself. For example, a typical DOS path might look like C:\text\letters\john.doc, where

the disc drive is C, the directory is called 'text', the subdirectory is called 'letters' and the file is called john.doc.

Path name See 'path'.

PC Personal Computer. Originally produced by IBM only, this computer has since been copied by many other manufacturers. The name 'PC' is commonly given to any generic desktop or portable computer, which is compatible with IBM's standards. PCs commonly use *OS/2 Warp*, DOS and/or Microsoft *Windows* as an operating system. Macintosh computers are not PCs, although the Power Macintosh range of computers are capable of running some PC software.

PCT Private Communication Technology. An upgrade to the SSL system for providing secure financial transactions on the Internet.

PEM A program for secure transmission of data across networks, which uses the RSA public-key encryption system.

Peripheral Generally a printer, plotter, scanner, CD-ROM or any other specialised piece of electronic hardware connected to a computer or network that provides a facility.

PGP Pretty Good Privacy. A program for secure transmission of data across networks, which uses the RSA public-key encryption system.

Pict A binary data format for storing pictures, mostly used by Macintoshes.

Platform Jargon for 'computer'. Hence, 'cross-platform integration' means making different types of computers work coherently together.

PoP Point of Presence. Internet providers and BBS companies provide modem users with phone numbers which they may dial, in order to connect their computers. Large operators provide numbers in major cities and rural areas, each of which is called a PoP.

Port This is the physical connection between your computer and any network or peripheral. If you look at the back of your computer, you should see at least one or two ports, which are in fact specialised sockets into which you can plug your network or peripheral cable. There are several types of ports, including serial, parallel and scsi.

Posting A contribution to one of the network news groups.

Postmaster A network system administrator who is responsible for e-mail facilities on his or her network.

PostScript A language / code used to send text and graphics to printers and plotters.

Power Macintosh A range of computers from Apple, capable of running many PC programs, as well as Macintosh programs. To be able to run such diverse software, a lot of code translation is required, and for this reason Power Macintoshes operate at very high speed. This also means that programs written specifically for the Power Macintosh can run very fast indeed.

PPP Point-to-Point Protocol. A protocol which enables the TCP/IP standard to be used over a serial link, such as a telephone line. Useful for modem users. Similar to SL/IP.

Privileges These are the individual 'rights' of a user on a multi-user computer or network, such as which files they may use, and which they may not, which printers they may use, and which they may not, etc.

Pro Short for 'professional'. This term is used to describe a piece of software, for which there is also a smaller, less advanced version, which has fewer functions, often called the 'lite' version. The 'pro' version of the software is often a commercial package, whereas the 'lite' version is often shareware or freeware.

Processor A silicon chip inside a computer that is designed to take incoming data, process it in some way, and output a result. See CPU.

Protocol A protocol is any set of rules and standards that define how a computer or a network should work. Many simple computer network languages are referred to as protocols.

Proxy An Internet host computer which acts as an intermediary between your computer and a remote Web site. Requests for Web documents are sent to the proxy. If the proxy does not already have that document in its cache, then it will retrieve the document from the remote Web site, keep a copy, and send a copy to your computer. If, shortly thereafter, the document is requested again by the same, or by another user of the proxy, the proxy's copy is sent rather than retrieving the document from the site of origin. Proxies will only keep documents for a short time, so there is little danger that out-of date versions of Web pages are sent. The use of proxies means that less long-distance requests for data are sent across the Internet, thus helping to reduce Internet traffic and the load on the Internet.

Public-key encryption A system for secure transmission of data across a network, which relies on the use of two 'digital' keys. Each user has their own private key and their own public key, but only the latter is transmitted across the network. Data may be encrypted using the public key, but may only be decoded by using both the public key and the private key. Hence data may only be unencrypted by the proper recipient.

Radio button A graphics symbol which has been designed to look like a button: usually a solid circle with an open circle around it. They can be 'pushed' on and off by pointing with the mouse and clicking the mouse button. They are found on some Web pages and many programs, and are used to select options.

RAM Random Access Memory. These are the silicon chips inside a computer that are used to store transient data. RAM only works whilst the power is on, so data needs to be saved onto a hard disc or other storage device, before the power is switched off. The amount of RAM a computer has is one measure of how 'powerful' it is. Compare with 'ROM'.

Remote computer Any computer you can access other than the one you are sitting in front of. 'Remote' may refer to the other side of the room you are in, or the other side of the World.

RFC Request For Comments. RFCs are documents that detail Internet protocols, and how the Internet is run. New RFCs are written by those who wish to make changes to the Internet, or to clarify certain aspects, and these may or may not be accepted by the various volunteer committees and work groups who help to manage the Internet.

ROM Read Only Memory. These are silicon chips inside a computer that are used to store data permanently. Data in ROM is not lost when the power is switched off. Data in ROM cannot be changed in any way. ROM is often used to store a very basic operating system for a computer, which immediately activates when the computer is switched on, so that the computer is then able to load the main operating system, such as *System 7* for a Macintosh, *Windows 95* or DOS for a PC. Compare with 'RAM' and 'CD-ROM'.

Router A computer within a network that controls the movement and forwarding of data and information 'packets'. The Internet has very many routers, that help to keep the electronic traffic moving.

RSA A popular 'public-key' encryption system used on the Internet for transmission of secure information, such as financial transactions. Developed by, and named after Ron Rivest, Adi Shamir, and Leonard Adleman, in 1977.

Scanner A electronic device which can scan a paper document and convert the image into binary code. With the right software, a scanner is a useful way of getting text and pictures into a computer system.

Seamless This describes a network, or suite of software packages, where the links have been cleverly disguised or hidden, so that the user is either wholly or partially unaware that there are any links at all. Thus the software or network appears much simpler and easier for the user, whilst remaining fully functional.

Search engine This is a program designed to find Web pages that relate to a subject specified by the user. There are several major search engine programs which may be accessed via the

Web. Simply enter one or more keywords into the search engine Web page, submit your request, and you will receive a new Web page with a list of links to Web pages that match your request. Each item is called a 'hit. You may also be able to choose the maximum number of 'hits' returned, and change other parameters which control how the search is conducted.

Self-extracting archive This is a special type of compressed computer file, which when executed, will decompress itself, without the need for special decompression programs. A self-extracting archive may produce one or more separate files or directories when it decompresses. Macintosh self-extracting archives are commonly found on Internet software archives and usually have the file name extension *.sea*. PC self-extracting archives have the file name extension .exe, although not all files with this file name extension are self-extracting archives. The .exe file name extension merely means that the file is an executable PC file.

Serial port This is a socket at the back of a computer that receives or transmits data a bit at a time. The serial port is also sometimes known as RS232. This socket on the back of a computer allows connection of an external modem, serial mouse and other peripherals. Compare with 'parallel port'.

Server Within a network, such as a LAN, it is common for one machine to be dedicated as a server. It does just that – serves the other computers on the network, handling routine network management, such as running printers and scanners. The server is also likely to have some large discs, which may be shared by other machines on the network. The server will be left running unattended most of the time, except when the system manager has to fix things. There are also many servers connected to the Internet that provide information to other computers on the Internet, such as Web pages.

SGML Standardised General Mark-up Language. A broad information standard for the encoding and structuring of information on computer systems. HTML is the SGML used on the Web.

Shareware Software which you can try before you buy it. Shareware is commonly available over the Internet. If you continue to use the software, you should register with the producers and must usually pay a small fee to them, or make a donation to a charity of their choice.

Shen A method for making data transfer via the Web reasonably secure, currently being developed at CERN. No PC or Macintosh implementations are currently available.

Site A computer (or computers) on the Internet which disseminates information. Web servers are often called sites, for example. The term is often applied to the specific organisation that controls the computer (or computers) in question.

SL/IP Serial Line / Internet Protocol. A protocol which enables the TCP/IP standard to be used over a serial link, such as a telephone line. Useful for modem users who wish to make a direct connection to the Internet. Similar to PPP.

SMTP Simple Mail Transfer Protocol. A method for sending e-mail across TCP/IP networks.

Snail mail A facetious term for regular mail sent via the post office. Used by e-mail addicts, it of course refers to the fact that regular mail is so much slower than e-mail.

Software This is the programming code that makes your hardware do something useful! Software can be stored temporarily in computer memory as long as the power is kept on, or more permanently on hard disc, diskettes, or CD-ROM. Software can also be transferred from computer to computer via networks such as the Internet.

Spam The act of posting commercial advertisements to Network News, irrespective of the relevance to the newsgroups involved. Spamming is frowned-upon by most users of the Internet, since it wastes users' time, as well as the resources and bandwidth of the Internet.

SSL Secure Sockets Layer. A system which provides secure transmission of data across TCP/IP networks such as the Internet. The layer of security sits between TCP/IP and the standard network protocols such as HTTP, FTP, SMTP, NNTP, Telnet, and Gopher. The system provides server authentication, encryption using the RSA system, and protection of data integrity.

STT Secure Transaction Technology. A relatively new system, more advanced than SSL, for secure financial transactions on the Internet, developed by Microsoft and Visa International.

Stateless A network program which will open a connection to another computer, only when it needs data from that other computer, and will close that connection immediately after the data has been transferred. This is in contrast to network programs which maintain a connection irrespective of whether data is being transferred. Programs which use HTTP, such as Web browsers, are stateless programs.

Surf The pastime of exploring what is available on the Internet, usually via the Web.

System 7 This is the operating system developed and used by Apple Computers for their range of Macintosh computers. A few people still use older versions, such as *System 6*, whilst more and more are using the latest version, which is currently System 7.5. Like Microsoft *Windows*, and IBM's *OS/2 Warp*, this operating system provides user-friendly windows, pull-down menus, icons and on-screen buttons. However, the system was developed by Apple well before Microsoft *Windows*, and IBM's *OS/2 Warp*.

Tag A code within HTML, the Hypertext Mark-up Language used to create Web pages. A Tag starts with the '<' character and ends with a '>', and does such things as control the appearance of text, allows the insertion of an image, or provides a hypertext link.

TCP/IP Transmission Control Protocol / Internet Protocol. This is a very widely used and fundamental collection of communication protocols utilised by the Internet, and many networked PCs and

Macintoshes. It is also used by a wide variety of other computer types.

Telco Telecommunications Company, e.g. British Telecom, AT&T, Bell etc.

Telnet A simple, but common TCP/IP protocol for accessing another computer remotely from your own, whether it be on the LAN or the Internet. Software which uses Telnet exists for most types of computer, such as the popular NCSA Telnet program. It effectively turns your computer into a terminal for the remote computer.

Text editor A program that allows a user to compose and edit a file of text. Word-processor programs are really just very sophisticated text editors.

The Net Abbreviation for the Internet.

Thumbnail A small image on a Web page which is linked to a larger version of the same image, which may be downloaded if required.

Transparent See 'seamless'.

Unix The most common operating system language on workstations such as those from Sun Microsystems and Silicon Graphics. It is also found on larger computers, but generally is not used on PCs and Macintoshes. You may well come across it if you log-in to a larger computer from your PC or Macintosh. Originally developed by AT&T, Unix has been around for many years and versions have been marketed by IBM, Unisys, SCO, Digital Equipment and Hewlett-Packard, amongst others.

Upload This is the process of moving or copying a file (i.e. data or program) from a smaller computer onto a larger computer. When you are connected to a large network, or bulletin board, you may be able to upload files from your PC or Macintosh.

URL Uniform Resource Locators. A standard way of describing the location of a file or other type of resource on the Internet, and its method of access.

Usenet An abbreviation for 'Users' Network'. A global network service for academic and commercial organisations which was started in the late 1970's. Its main role now is to provide a conferencing system, better known as Network News.

User A person who uses something, such as a computer or computer program.

Username The unique identity code for each person who is registered on a multi-user computer or network. A username usually comprises alphanumeric characters that bear some relation to the user's real name.

UUencode Unix to Unix encode. A method for coding any file using ASCII characters only (i.e. text). Particularly used within Network News.

UUNET A non-profit network designed to provide access to USENET Network News, various computer archives, and e-mail facilities.

Veronica Very Easy Rodent-Orientated Net-wide Index to Computerised Archives (normally spelled with a lower-case 'v'). A program written at the University of Nevada which permits keyword searches to be done on Gopher information servers.

Virus A program which is usually quite small, is able to replicate itself, and when activated, can cause problems, ranging from printing irritating messages on the screen, to the full-scale destruction of a hard disc. Virus programs are written by anti-social programmers around the world. Viruses are most commonly transmitted from one computer to another on diskettes, and via the Internet. Diskettes and computers that have a virus on them are said to be 'infected'. Viruses can only be activated if they are executed, so only executable files are liable to infection. So, for example, e-mail messages cannot be infectious. To combat viruses, always have an anti-virus program installed on your computer, learn how to use it, and use it regularly.

VMS A computer operating system developed for Vax mainframe computers. It is now less popular than the rival Unix operating system. It is generally not used on PCs and Macintoshes, but

you may well come across it if you log-in to a larger computer from your PC or Macintosh. IBM DOS was originally developed from VMS, so that now, IBM DOS, Microsoft DOS and Novell DOS all have many commands in common with VMS, such as DIR, CD, DEL, and many others.

VT100 Historically, this was originally a widely used type of computer terminal manufactured by the Digital Equipment Corporation. It was a primitive monochrome text-only display. The format of the VT100 screen has since become a kind of standard display type. Many different kinds of computers can emulate the VT100, including PCs and Macintoshes, provided they have the right software. This is important for increased compatibility. It is particularly used for Telnet sessions.

WAIS Wide Area Information Servers. A way of locating and extracting files from large databases, such as those found on the Internet. WAIS searches for files using keywords which the user enters.

WAN Wide Area Network. A computer network that may be national or global in extent, and which may use a variety of communication links, such as dedicated electrical or optical cables, telephone lines, radio or satellite links. Most WANs are used in the commercial environment.

WIT Web Interactive Talk. This is a Web-based conference or discussion group, in which registered Web users may contribute information and make queries. Text is submitted using Web forms. The system is comparable to Network News and IRC (Internet Relay Chat), but is entirely Web dependent.

W3 See World Wide Web.

Web See World Wide Web.

White pages directory A computer database containing people's e-mail addresses, and possibly also postal addresses, telephone numbers, etc. If the database is on the Internet it is usually easily accessible via Gopher or World Wide Web.

Windows A window is a rectangular area, usually with some graphical scrolling devices at the sides, and a menu bar at the top, which allows you to control your computer or run a program. Most computers allow the user to operate the computer via one or more windows, which may be displayed on the screen at the same time, and which may overlap one another. Macintosh computers have always used windows, via an operating system developed by Apple Computers, currently called *System 7*. Window systems have now become very popular on the PC also, especially Microsoft *Windows* and *Windows 95*, which is what is often meant by people who use the term 'windows'. A rival PC windows operating system is produced by IBM, called *OS/2 Warp*.

World Wide Web Also known as the Web, WWW and W3. This is a hypertext system for storing and retrieving data on any network that uses the network communication standard, TCP/IP. The Web was originally developed at CERN, the European Centre for Particle Physics, between 1989 and 1991. The Web uses the HTML code to create pages of text and images, and link these to sound files and video clip files, as well as other Web pages. Web pages are stored and retrieved via a network using the TCP/IP communication language HTTP.

WWW See World Wide Web.

WYSIWYG What You See Is What You Get. Pronounced 'wiz-ee-wig'. A term applied to text and graphic editor programs which display on-screen the exact appearance of the final output, whilst you carry out editing. Most good, modern editors tend to be WYSIWYG. Microsoft *Word* is a good example of a WYSIWYG wordprocessor program. Non-WYSIWYG programs do not allow you to see the appearance of the final output whilst you are in editing mode, and are less common today. *WordPerfect* was originally entirely a non-WYSIWYG word-processor program, since whilst editing, the user could see all the control codes on screen, as well as ordinary text.

X.500 Developed by the CCITT (Comite Consultatif International Telegraphique et Telephonique), this is a network protocol specifically designed to handle large databases that are distributed across a network of computers. It is widely used for large address, telephone and e-mail directories.

Appendix 2

SOFTWARE SUPPLIERS

Apple Computers Ltd
6 Roundwood Avenue
Stockley Park
Uxbridge
Middlesex, UB11 1BB

URL: *http://www.apple.com/*
E-MAIL: *webmaster@apple.com*

ARTA Software Group
Suite H201
15520 Mill Creek Blvd.
Mill Creek, WA 98012
USA

URL: *http://www.halcyon.com/webwizard/*
E-MAIL: *davidg@arta.com*

BBEdit HTML Extensions
E-MAIL: *infosys@si.uji.es*
URL: *http://www.uji.es/bbedit-html-extensions.html*

Brooklyn North Software Works
25 Doyle Street
Bedford
Nova Scotia, B4A 1K4
Canada

URL: *http://fox.nstn.ca/~harawitz/index.html*
E-MAIL: *sales@brooknorth.bedford.ns.ca*

Cornell Law School
Legal Information Institute
Ithaca
New York
USA

URL: *http://www.law.cornell.edu/cello/cellotop.html*
E-MAIL: *lii@fatty.law.cornell.edu*

Tradewave
3636 Executive Center Drive
Austin
Texas 78731
USA

URL: *http://galaxy.einet.net/EINet/EINet.html*
E-MAIL: *info@einet.net*

Excel 5.0 to HTML Converter
Jordan Evans
NASA Goddard Space Flight Center
Greenbelt
Maryland 20771
USA

URL: *http://rs712b.gsfc.nasa.gov/704/dgd/xl2html.html*
E-MAIL: *jordan.evans@gsfc.nasa.gov*

HTML Writer
Kris Nosack
Computer Integrated Manufacturing (CIM)
Brigham Young University
Provo
Utah
USA

URL: *http://lal.cs.byu.edu/people/nosack/*
E-MAIL: *html-writer@byu.edu*

IBM
National Enquiry Centre
Mailpoint F3M
P.O. Box 41
North Harbour
Portsmouth
Hampshire, P06 3AU

URL: *http://www.ibm.com/*
E-MAIL: *askibm@info.ibm.com*

InterCon Systems Corporation
950 Herndon Parkway
Herndon, VA 22070
USA

URL: *http://www.intercon.com/*
E-MAIL: *sales@intercon.com*

Internet Software Technologies
P.O. Box 756
28 Squire Street
Sackville
New Brunswick
E0A 3C0
Canada

URL: *http://www.ist.ca/*
E-MAIL: *sales@ist.ca*

KnowledgeWorks Incorporated
Suite A-141
2251 San Diego Ave.
San Diego, CA 92110
USA

URL: *http://www.nesbitt.com/*
E-MAIL: *webedit@thegroup.net*

MediaTech Incorporated
9785 Shenandoah Dr.
Cleveland
Ohio 44141-2833
USA

URL: *http://www.mediatec.com/*
E-MAIL:*webmaster@mediatec.com*

Microsoft Ltd.
Microsoft Place
Winnersh
Wokingham
Berkshire, RG11 5TP

URL: *http://www.microsoft.com/*
E-MAIL: *saleinfo@microsoft.com*

National Center for Supercomputing Applications
University of Illinois
Champagne
Illinois
USA

URL: *http://www.ncsa.uiuc.edu/General/NCSAHome.html*
E-MAIL: *orders@ncsa.uiuc.edu.*

Netscape Communications Corporation
Suite 500
650 Castro Street
Mountain View
California, 94041
USA

URL: *http://home.netscape.com/*
URL: *ftp://ftpx.netscape.com*   (where *x* is a digit from 2–8)
E-MAIL: *info@netscape.com*

Sausage Software
Griffo - IDeA
Sausage European Distribution
Burggravenlaan 20
B-9000 Gent
Belgium

URL: *http://www.netpoint.be/shop/hotdog/*
E-MAIL: *idea@netpoint.be*

SoftQuad Incorporated
56 Aberfoyle Crescent
Toronto
Ontario
M8X 2W4
Canada

URL: *http://www.sq.com/*
E-MAIL: *mail@sq.com*

SPRY Incorporated
Suite 200
316 Occidental Avenue South
Seattle
Washington 98104
USA

URL: *http://www.spry.com/index.html*
E-MAIL: *info26@spry.com*

Spyglass Incorporated
Suite 304
1230 East Diehl Road
Naperville
Illinois 60563
USA

URL: *http://www.spyglass.com/*
E-MAIL: *mosaic@spyglass.com*

Trumpet Software International Pty Ltd
GPO Box 1649
Hobart
Tasmania, 7001
Australia

URL: *http://www.trumpet.com.au/home.htm*
E-MAIL: *info@trumpet.com.au*

Appendix 3

INTERNET VENDORS

Atlas InterNet Ltd.
19 Devonshire St
London, W1N 1FS

URL: *http://www.atlas.co.uk/atlas/default.htm*
E-MAIL: *postmaster@atlas.co.uk*

CityScape Internet Services Ltd.
Alexandria House
Covent Garden
Cambridge, CB1 3JE

URL: *http://www.cityscape.co.uk/*
E-MAIL: *sales@cityscape.co.uk*

Compulink Information Exchange (CIX)
Suite 2, The Sanctuary
Oakhill Grove
Surbiton
Surrey, KT6 6DU

URL: *http://www.compulink.co.uk/*
E-MAIL: *cixadmin@cix.compulink.co.uk*

CompuServe
1 Redcliff Street
P.O. Box 676
Bristol, BS99 1YN

URL: *http://compuserve.com/index.html*
E-MAIL: *sales@cis.compuserve.com*

Connect BBS
P.O. Box 360
Harrow, HA1 4LQ

URL: *http://www.ibmpcug.co.uk/*
E-MAIL: *info@ibmpcug.co.uk*

Demon Internet Ltd.
Gateway House
322 Regents Park Road
Finchley
London, N3 2QQ

URL: *http://www.demon.co.uk/*
E-MAIL: *sales@demon.net*

EUnet GB
Wilson House
John Wilson Business Park
Whitstable
Kent, CT5 3QY

URL: *http://www.britain.eu.net/*
E-MAIL: *sales@Britain.EU.net*

eWorld
Apple Computer UK Ltd.
6 Roundwood Avenue
Stockley Park
Uxbridge
Middlesex, UB11 1BB

URL: *http://www.eworld.com/*
E-MAIL: *subscribe@eworld.com*

Frontier Internet Service Ltd.
1st Floor
45 Hatton Garden
London, EC1N 8EX

URL: *http://www.ftech.net/*
E-MAIL: *info@ftech.net*

Hiway
Compass Computer Group Ltd.
Unity House
Kennetside
Newbury
Berkshire, RG14 5PX

URL: *http://www.hiway.co.uk/*
E-MAIL: *info@inform.hiway.co.uk*

IBM Global Network
National Enquiry Centre
Mailpoint F3M
P.O. Box 41
North Harbour
Portsmouth
Hampshire, P06 3AU

URL: *http://www.ibm.com/globalnetwork/glohome.htm*
E-MAIL: *inquire@uk.ibm.com*

RedNet Ltd
6 Cliveden Office Village
Lancaster Road
High Wycombe
Buckinghamshire, HP12 3YZ

URL: *http://www.rednet.co.uk/*
E-MAIL: *orders@rednet.co.uk*

The Direct Connection
P O Box 931
London, SE18 3PW

URL: *http://www.dircon.co.uk/*
E-MAIL: *sales@dircon.co.uk*

The Microsoft Network
Microsoft Ltd.
Microsoft Place
Winnersh
Wokingham
Berkshire, RG11 5TP

URL: *http://www.msn.com/*
E-MAIL: *saleinfo@microsoft.com*

Unipalm PIPEX Ltd.
216 Cambridge Science Park
Cambridge, CB4 4WA

URL: *http://www.unipalm.pipex.com/*
E-MAIL: *info@unipalm.pipex.com*

Index

A

anchor 9, 175
Aliweb 103
anonymous FTP 85, 175
Apple Computers 15, 16, 107, 175
application 175
  helper 52
ARA 17, 18, 31, 173
Archie 175
Arcnet,
ARPANET 3, 176
ASCII 78, 85, 176
attachment 78
authoring 176

B

'Bad Request 400' 42
backbone 3, 176
backlink 9, 176
bandwidth 176
baud 176
BBS 2, 16, 22, 176
binary 73, 85, 177
BinHex 72, 78, 88, 90, 177
bit 177
bit-map 177
BITNET 177
Bookmark 48-50, 177
BPS 176, 177
browser 5, 14, 20, 25-28, 32, 157, 178
  Cello 163
  customisation of browsers 27
  IBM WebExplorer 161
  MacWeb 163
  Microsoft Internet Explorer 161
  NCSA Mosaic 159
  Netscape Navigator 19, 157
  Spry Air Mosaic 160
  Spyglass Enhanced Mosaic 161
  winWeb 163
bug 159, 178
Bulletin Board System, *see* BBS
Button 37, 178
byte 178

C

cache 45-48, 178
card 9, 10, 178
case 31, 80, 178
CD-ROM 11, 12, 179
CERN 4, 8, 179
checkbox 37, 38, 179
CIX 179
clickable maps 55, 179
client computer 12, 13, 33, 173, 179
client program 13, 179
clipboard 180
Compuserve 2, 16, 107, 180
conference 180
CPU 180
Crash 46, 159, 180
cryptography 63
cyberspace 141, 153, 180

D

daemon 181
DARPA 3
data 33, 173, 181
database 181
decompression 26, 89, 90
device 181
dialogue box 181
directory 27, 181
disc cache 45-47, 181
disc drive 87, 181
diskette 182
DNS 28, 182
domain 182
Domain Name Server 182
DOS 182
download 33, 45, 46, 54, 182

E

e-cash 112, 182
e-mail 3, 4, 77-83, 160, 182
  attachments 78
  enclosures 78
  etiquette 82
  mailbox name 79
  mailto 80
e-text 183
electronic mail, *see* e-mail
encryption 63-66, 183
  public-key 64, 198
error codes 42
Ethernet 2, 183
E-zine 141, 142, 183

F

FAQ 75, 183
file 86, 183
file extension 30, 57, 60, 87, 90, 183
File Transfer Protocol, *see* FTP
firewall 34, 35, 184
flame 76, 183
floppy disc 93, 184
font 50, 184
'Forbidden 403' 42

218

Notes

Notes

Notes

Notes